Mummy
is a Killer

WALTHA

D0522785

904

Mummy is a Killer

Her little brother and sister were dead and
the woman she loved most was to blame

Nikkia Roberson

EBURY
PRESS

7 9 10 8

This edition published 2012
First published in 2012 by Ebury Press,
an imprint of Ebury Publishing
A Random House Group company

Copyright © Nikkia Roberson 2012

Nikkia Roberson has asserted her right to be identified as the
author of this Work in accordance with the Copyright,
Designs and Patents Act 1988

This work has been co-written with Katy Weitz

Extract on pages 128–130 from Newsday © 20 Oct 1999. All rights
reserved. Used by permission and protected by the Copyright Laws of
the United States. The printing, copying, redistribution or retransmiss-
ion of the Material without express written permission is prohibited

All rights reserved. No part of this publication may be reproduced,
stored in a retrieval system, or transmitted in any form or by any
means, electronic, mechanical, photocopying, recording or otherwise,
without the prior permission of the copyright owner

The Random House Group Limited Reg. No. 954009

Addresses for companies within the Random House Group
can be found at www.randomhouse.co.uk

A CIP catalogue record for this book is available from the British Library

ISBN 9780091949709

To buy books by your favourite authors and register for offers visit
www.randomhouse.co.uk

Penguin Random House is committed to a sustainable future for
our business, our readers and our planet. This book is made from
Forest Stewardship Council® certified paper.

Printed and bound in Great Britain by Clays Ltd, St Ives plc

This book is a work of non-fiction based on the life, experiences and recollections of the author. The names of some people, places, dates, sequences or the details of events may have been changed to protect the privacy of others.

Waltham Forest Libraries	
904 000 00457370	
Askews & Holts	17-Jun-2016
364.1523 ROB	£7.99
5062981	

Those we Love remain with us
For Love itself lives on.
Cherished memories never fade
Because a loved one is gone.
Those we Love can never be
More than a thought apart.
For as long as there is memory
They'll live on in our heart.

– Author Unknown

Forgiveness is the final form of Love.

– Reinhold Neibuhr

Contents

Prologue

SOMETIMES I LOOK at my hands and I smile. They are my mom's hands – long, tapering fingers that wrinkle and crease at the knuckles. They turn up at the ends so when I stretch them out they look like an opened flower. I am like my mom in so many ways – we have the same round dark eyes, the same smile and laugh. We walk the same too. Sometimes I look at other women together in the street and you can tell they are moms and daughters – they look alike. I want that. I want to walk down the street with my mom, arm in arm, looking the same. I want everyone to see we are related.

But I don't have that. I don't have anyone like me out there.

Most of the time I feel very alone in the world. I want to do the things other moms and daughters do – go to the mall, go out for dinner, laugh and talk together.

But I don't know if I'll ever have that. You see, my mom is locked up in a mental institution. I don't know if she's ever going to get out. But I hope one day she does.

I used to be scared of her hands. I used to look at

them and wonder how on earth they did what they did. I wondered if my hands were the same; if I could do what she did. I've spent many years wondering and worrying about how similar we are. And what that similarity might mean for me.

This is the story of how I learned to love my mom, her hands, and mine.

1

Locked Out

'I WANNA GO inside!' Momo whined, sticking out her bottom lip in frustration and tugging at the front of her shorts.

'Yeah, me too but we can't! So you'll just have to wait,' I told her patiently. It was a hot summer's day in Brentwood, New York and the cars slid lazily past our front lawn as we three kids sat around, waiting for the front door to open.

We'd been outside since midday and time seemed to have slowed to a standstill as the baking sun beat down on our bare legs and arms.

I scratched absent-mindedly at a scab on my elbow while I tried to work out how long we'd been out there.

The sun had moved way over in the sky and long shadows were beginning to creep up the side of the house.

As usual, Mom had put us out when her friends arrived, and although we could hear their voices inside and see their faces occasionally appear at the window to check we were still out there, nobody let us in.

I looked down at my little sister Momo as she danced from one foot to the other in her pink jelly sandals. Her real name was Delvin but everyone had called her Momo since she was a baby because her middle name was Monae.

'You wanna pee?' I asked. 'You know you can't pee on yourself or Mom will get mad and give you a whooping!' I warned her.

'I don't care,' Momo replied sulkily, though behind her defiance I could see fear – she didn't want to end up with wet shorts *and* a whooping.

But Momo wasn't one to back down easily. Out of the three of us, she was the difficult one, always acting up, answering back, and right now she was giving me that angry, rebellious look.

'Look – pee round the side of the house, like I did,' I told her firmly. 'Just go round the side and squat down there. They're not gonna let us in anytime soon.'

So Momo hopped off round the side to relieve herself while I held our little brother Mellie's hand.

As far back as I can remember Mellie and Momo were always there. At five, I was just a year older than my sister Momo, four, and she was a year older than our three-year-old brother Mellie, so it was always the three of us. And if Mom wasn't around I was in charge.

'You wanna pee too?' I asked Mellie, who had his thumb stuck in his mouth. His real name was Melvin but he was always Mellie to us.

Mellie shook his head. He was a sweetie, never demanded anything, never got mad or cried. Mellie would just do whatever he was told, never complaining or making a fuss, unlike Momo, who kicked up a stink all the time. Those two, they were as different as night and day.

'You thirsty?' I asked, feeling the dryness scratch the back of my own throat.

He nodded. We hadn't had anything to eat or drink since lunchtime when Mom gave us ham and cheese sandwiches and soda.

So I took him to the hose next to the steps at the front of the house and turned on the tap, careful to hold my finger over the top so the water wouldn't come out too fast. Mellie tipped his face to one side and opened his mouth obediently as the water shot into it and he made catlike lapping motions with his tongue.

Meanwhile, Momo reappeared from the side of the house, hitching up her jean shorts and shouting: 'Me too! Wait for me!'

I turned the hose in her direction, pushed both thumbs into the top and let her have it!

'Hey!' she shouted as the droplets hit her head and clothes, giggling and running back out to the lawn, away from my attack.

After we'd all taken turns drinking from the outside hose we played with my dolls, giving them a tea party. Every half an hour or so one of us would knock on the front door, trying to entice my mom or one of the adults to open up.

'Hey, come on – we're hungry!' Momo yelled into the crack of the door opening.

'Mom? Mom? Will ya let us in now, please? *Please?*'

After a while we swapped to playing 'School'. I was the teacher of course and if anybody was naughty I'd give them a smack. When we tired of playing School we played House – I was the mommy, my sister Momo was the daddy and my brother Mellie was the baby.

And if anyone was naughty I'd give them a smack!

When everyone had got thoroughly annoyed with my smacking, Mellie wandered off to play with his cars while Momo and I bickered over whose turn it was to be the mommy.

Finally, we just sat on the apartment steps, too tired and hungry to play as the sun slunk behind the tower blocks in our street and the sky turned a hazy tangerine.

Then, the key turned in the door and Mom's face appeared, her eyes heavy-lidded and glazed.

'Come on!' she yelled. 'Get in here now!'

Surprised but pleased we scrambled to our feet and scampered up the steps to the house.

The overpowering smell of incense struck us as soon as we got in the front door but we didn't care. We headed straight for the kitchen where I turned out some packet noodles into three bowls and heated them up in the microwave.

The three of us sat at the kitchen table gobbling down our noodles while Mom said a lingering, slow goodbye to her friends.

As soon as we'd had our fill, Mom hurried us to bed. I helped the other two get into their pyjamas then me, Mellie and Momo clambered to the top of our red metal-framed bunk bed and hunkered down together under the covers, exhausted from our day outside and relieved to finally be in our own bed.

Curled up together, Mellie on one side and Momo on the other, with the comforting pressure of their bodies on mine, I could feel their little chests rise and fall as their breathing deepened and they both fell asleep. Then I let myself drift off too.

Looking back, those were good times with my brother Mellie and sister Momo, though we had no idea we were being neglected.

I was only five, so it never occurred to me that other kids didn't get locked out of their house for hours on end while their moms entertained friends.

Much later I learned that Mom was a drug addict and dealer. Her 'friends' were people who would come round to our house to smoke crack or heroin and of course nobody wanted a bunch of kids getting in the way, so we were left outside to fend for ourselves.

God knows what the neighbours made of seeing us three little kids sitting outside their homes for hours at a time, but I guess nobody made a fuss because we were left to get on with it.

Some of the people who came to hang out with my mom were normal – some even brought along their own kids who got left outside with us to play while they smoked drugs and lit incense sticks to cover the smell.

Others were strange. I remember this one lady who dressed in dirty boys clothes and had a raspy voice. She always rode up on her bicycle and said weird things to me – I didn't like her at all. I may have been young, but at five years old I was already pretty streetwise. After all, I spent a lot of the time out on the street.

But on the whole, we didn't pay much attention to the people who were coming and going from the house. Our world consisted of each other, Mom, Grandma, who we'd go to visit, and Mom's new husband Beanie.

I called him Beanie, but I'm pretty sure that wasn't his real name – it's just what everyone called him. Although I didn't know it at the time, he wasn't my real dad, only Mellie and Momo's dad.

Beanie acted like he loved us – he was affectionate and hugged us – but he was also a drug addict and he and my mom got into some bad fights sometimes. I'd hear them screaming at each other while they were both high, letting out a whole bunch of curses and spitting angrily into each other's faces. They'd go at it over any old thing and when I heard their voices rising, I'd take Mellie and Momo off to our room because it looked ugly and mean and I didn't want the little ones getting scared.

'Come on,' I'd say. 'Let's play House!' And sometimes it wasn't make-believe, I really was their mommy looking after them.

Mom and Beanie weren't the only ones who fought a lot – some of my mom's friends got into some horrible fights at our house too. I remember one time this lady had a broom and she pushed this other woman against the kitchen door with it at her neck. I didn't know what they were fighting about but it sure didn't look nice.

Yup, there were definitely times we were relieved to be sent out to play in the front yard.

We loved Mom – of course we did. She was our mom and she was real pretty and had nice hair. And Mom could be wonderful – bubbly, excitable and with a terrific laugh, one that sounded like the flow of water down the side of a mountain. She could be the most fun person to be around. She loved to play her reggae music on the stereo and dance around with us in her bedroom.

Our mom was a great dancer and Momo and I would swing our hips about and throw our arms in the air, trying to mimic her fluid moves.

And there were times she took us out to the front lawn herself to play tea parties. She had her own bunch of dolls and sometimes she let us play with them but we weren't allowed to touch them when she wasn't there.

But there was another side to Mom, an angry, mean side. I remember how her eyes looked when she was mad and high – like she was possessed.

You didn't want to be near Mom when she was like that, it was like she was crazy, out of her mind.

If we were naughty or we acted up then she'd take a belt to us and whoop us real hard.

I don't think she meant to hurt us as bad as she did but at the time it looked like she didn't know what she was doing.

She'd get that belt and bring it down hard on my back, butt and legs a whole bunch of times. I'd be trying to run away, squirming all round the room so eventually she'd have me locked in an unbreakable grip, her finger-nails digging painfully into my thin arms, as she worked the belt with the other hand.

I could tell if Mom was herself or if she was in one of her 'strange moods'. It was a form of self-preservation learned from a very young age but it now became instinctive. The signs were subtle but they were defi-nitely there. The way she talked, her laugh, even the way she walked changed. Everything about her would be faster, higher, more intense. You couldn't pin her down, get a straight answer out of her or make her sit still. It's like she was on fast-forward.

There were times when it would be obvious to anyone. Mom would talk to people who weren't there, pace the floor, sit with her legs shaking madly or turn suddenly to look over her shoulder, as if something had just disturbed her. She'd start to talk about God or the devil and she'd get her Bible out and start reading scriptures from it over and over.

It was like she was somewhere else entirely. I could tell it wasn't right because I could see the way other people acted when she was like that. Beanie didn't want to be around her when she was acting crazy and other people looked at her funny.

'Whatchoo doin'?' I'd ask her when she was in one of her moods, crossing herself or talking to imaginary people.

But she wouldn't answer. It was as if she couldn't even hear me.

We had no set routine in Brentwood and Mom never put us in day care so we just got up and did what we wanted, when we wanted.

The only time we got settled into something close to a routine was when Mom dropped us off at Grandma's house.

Annie, my grandma, was my mom's mom, and lived just a half mile from us in a big house on Coconut Street with my grandpa Willie. I loved her so much that every time we visited I never wanted to leave.

My grandma came from the South originally, a place called Augusta in Georgia, and she was raised on good, wholesome Southern food. She made the best macaroni cheese in the world and she had cool toys and bikes at her house.

Their place was always clean and tidy and she never locked us outside.

Sometimes Mom would drop us off in the morning and turn up to collect us late at night, when Grandma would have to rouse us out of sleep to get us to go home.

'Why didn't you come earlier?' I'd hear my grandma hissing to my mom as they struggled down the corridor, each carrying a heavy, dozing child.

Silence.

Grandma would try again. 'Where you been all this time? I called and called and you never picked up the phone.'

'I've been out,' Mom would finally reply. 'Anyways, don't bother me none about it now. Just help me with the kids, would you?'

Sometimes Mom would fail to turn up for two or three days at a time.

When she'd finally appear I'd be so happy and comfortable at Grandma's I wouldn't want to go home.

'No, don't make me! Please, Grandma. I just wanna stay with you!' I'd cry tearfully to my grandma, holding on to her skirts as my mom hopped impatiently from one foot to the other, scowling in my direction.

'Hush now!' Grandma would soothe. 'You can come back and visit again soon.'

But above me I could hear her whisper to my mom, 'Why does this girl cry like this all the time? It's not normal for a child to cry like this when it's time to go home.'

None of us ever told Grandma about being left outside for hours on end or the beatings. It's not because we were warned not to, it just didn't occur to us that any mom treated their kids any different.

It was nicer at Grandma's house. She didn't have strange friends, the wallpaper wasn't peeling off her walls and she cooked good food. She even had a pool in her backyard and I got to know some of the other kids on the block so I made friends in the area.

We would ride our bikes up and down the road and play Tag. Then Grandma would call us in for dinner where we'd wolf down home-made macaroni choose, fried chicken and collard greens.

I'd dread hearing my mom's car pull up to pick us all up and take us back to our place in Brentwood.

But then there was the time when she finally arrived to pick us up. She had left us at Grandma's for a whole week and the car was full of stuff.

'We ain't going back to Brentwood today,' she told us. 'And there ain't going to be any more Beanie. We've got a new home now!'

2
Belport

OUR NEW APARTMENT was in a homeless shelter in north Belport, Long Island, New York. It was quite a drive from Grandma's but not too far if we ever needed her.

I guess there had been one too many rows. Beanie had left Mom and without his income she couldn't afford to keep up the house in Brentwood so we had to move into a shelter for homeless families.

It looked pretty nice from the outside. There were several large two-storey apartment blocks where the families lived, all laid out in a semicircle around a park in the middle.

Dotted around the park were benches, streetlights and even a small playground where us kids could play – there were loads of other kids around so Mellie and Momo and I quickly made friends.

Our apartment was good too. Momo and I liked jumping on the beds. One time we got carried away jumping and shouting when we were supposed to be taking our naps.

'Okay – which one of you is going first?' Mom

bellowed as she strode into the room, a belt wrapped menacingly round her fist.

Momo and I were mid-jump when she came in but as soon as I saw the belt, I bolted back into the corner of the room.

Momo stood still, just where she'd landed on the bed, almost daring my mom to beat her first.

So she did.

And it looked like it was a bad one. I could see Momo clenching her teeth and her face reddening from the pain as Mom thwacked the back of her bare legs over and over again, but she never made a sound.

Afterwards, she got off the bed and stood in front of Mom, her hands on her hips, lips quivering but her chin pushed upwards.

'That didn't hurt,' she bragged, though I could see Mom had walloped her pretty hard. That was Momo for you – so defiant!

While it killed me to hear her bringing down so much pain on herself, at the same time I admired her courage. I could never have said the things she said. She was only four and she had so much spirit!

'Oh no?' said Mom, disappearing into the hallway and reappearing seconds later with a bigger, meaner-looking belt. 'Well, let's see if you've still got a smart mouth after I give you a whooping with this one. I'll teach you to answer me back, young lady!'

And with that she set upon Momo really bad.

Afterwards Momo didn't say anything. She inched herself gingerly off Mom's lap and hobbled over to where I was standing. Then it was my turn.

It hurt all right and I just let the tears tumble down my face but it wasn't half as hard as Momo's.

'Now lie down the both of you and take your damn naps like I told you!' Mom snarled as she left the room.

Momo and I lay face down on the bed – my face already blotchy and puffed up from crying. But Momo held it all in.

Finally, when the door slammed shut Momo let a great big sob escape.

There was another game we liked to play in Belport – it was called Go Hide!

It wasn't really a game as such but me, Mellie and Momo thought it was real fun, so it might as well have been a game.

Occasionally, people used to come knocking on the door and Mom would shout at us to: 'Go Hide!' and we all used to have to squeeze in a corner together so that the people at the door didn't know we were home.

Even Mom would scrunch up against us in the corner and we all found it so funny we'd start giggling. Mom would be trying to shush us. 'Y'all, come on, hurry up. Shhh! Y'all be quiet now.'

The people at the door would keep knocking and

knocking but we'd just stay hidden in the corner so they couldn't see or hear us.

To this day I have no idea who those people were who came knocking on our door. Maybe it was Child Protective Services, maybe it was the cops or some more drug addicts wanting a hit.

Maybe it was Beanie or maybe it was my grandma.

I don't know – all I know is that sometimes we'd all pretend there was nobody home, even when there were four of us there.

Mom's drug taking got pretty bad at Belport and she wound up leaving us with another family at the shelter quite a lot while she went out for hours.

Our apartment was in a block on one side of the semicircle and the other family lived on the same floor in the opposite block all the way round the other side. If you opened our door, you could wave to them on the other side!

They had a five-year-old daughter, Jess, who we liked to play with, and when we first got to Belport the wife was heavily pregnant with another baby.

I was looking forward to the baby being born so I could go over and cuddle it. I loved babies, more than anything in the world.

One day, just a few weeks after moving into Belport, Mom left us at Jess's again while her mom was in the hospital having had her little boy.

That morning Jess and her dad showed us all the pictures they'd taken in the hospital of her little brother – he looked so cute. I was really jealous but excited at the same time. Soon he'd be home and I'd be able to hold him too.

We had our lunch and it was naptime. Mellie, Momo and Jess were asleep on the big bed in the main bedroom while I lay down on the floor by the side of the bed.

I can't have been asleep because I noticed the bedroom door opening and Jess's dad tiptoeing silently into the room and lying down next to me.

Before he'd said a word, he thrust his hand down the front of my shorts.

I was too surprised to say or do anything. I didn't understand what was going on or why. I was frozen, too terrified to move or shout.

He started rubbing me up and down, which hurt quite bad, but I didn't say anything.

After a while the pain got worse so I tried to edge backwards and get away from his hand but I was stuck, wedged between his large body and the bed, where my little brother and sister lay sleeping behind me.

It didn't go on for long – he had his other hand down the front of his own pants and eventually he shuddered, drew back his hand and let out a long sigh.

Then he gave me this serious look and said: 'If you tell anyone about this I'll do it again.'

I was frightened – I didn't want to tell anyone.

That night when my mom came to collect us I practically ran back to our apartment. I felt sore down below and upset from what Jess's dad had done to me at naptime but I don't think anyone noticed my strange mood.

But later that evening, in the bath, Mom obviously saw something that didn't look right.

'Somebody been touching you?' she asked sharply.

I froze all over again. I didn't know what she'd seen, whether it was a scratch or a sore or whether I was somehow marked from the assault, but I was terrified of telling her what had happened.

If I told, he'd do it to me again! What if it was worse next time? What if he really hurt me?

I looked down, splashing the water up around my legs, trying to cover the evidence of what was clearly a sexual assault on a five-year-old.

'I ... ah ... I err ... I don't want to say,' I whimpered in a small voice.

I felt guilty, as if I'd done something wrong, and Mom's accusatory tone didn't help much. Sitting there in that bath, my limbs skinny and bare, I felt so small, so vulnerable.

'You tell Mommy!' Mom ordered, her voice rising with emotion. 'You tell Mommy right this minute! Somebody been touching you down there?'

'I don't want to tell you,' I repeated. As long as I

didn't say anything then I wasn't lying and nobody would get hurt.

But Mom wasn't taking no for an answer. She started to get really angry with me. 'Oh yes you are!' she said. 'You are going to tell me what happened. Yes you are, Madam – otherwise you are gonna get a whooping from Mommy. A real big whooping!'

She yanked me out of the bath, threw a towel around me and made me sit on the edge of the bed.

'Come on, now – tell Momma!' she said, adopting a lighter, conciliatory tone.

But I just shook my head and clamped my lips together.

'Well now, you can just sit there and wait till you're ready to talk!'

And that's where she left me for an hour while she bustled angrily around the apartment, putting my brother and sister in the bath, and checking each of them for signs.

She seemed relieved they didn't appear to exhibit any evidence of assault but it didn't do much to quell her anger. She kept returning to the bed, threatening to whoop me.

'Please, Mom,' I whined. 'Please can I just put my pyjamas on and watch TV?'

'No!' she shot back. 'Not a chance! You're not moving till you tell me what happened.'

Eventually she did as threatened and she whooped me with a belt.

Finally the tears came streaming down my face and there in her bedroom, the towel wrapped round my still naked and sore body, I poured out the whole story to her.

I don't think she'd wanted to hurt me more – I don't think she was thinking at all. She was just really mad at this point – mad at the person who had hurt her child. And now she was mad at me for protecting him. She didn't know any other way to get me to open my mouth and turn the guy in.

But sometimes I do wonder – did she realise what she was doing? Beating a little girl the same day she'd been molested?

I don't remember Mom being any nicer to me afterwards; she was still as mad as hell.

She called the cops of course and I got sent to the doctor, who had to look at me down there, which was really embarrassing. He even looked inside me, which was horrible, really uncomfortable.

A few days later the police went to arrest Jess's dad. It was awful. I watched the whole scene unfold from our front windows. From the other side of the semicircle I could see the uniformed officers talking to Jess's mom, who was home from hospital. She was holding the new baby and looking really confused and upset, then she started getting mad and shouting. Then they barged past her and she disappeared back inside after them.

They were back outside minutes later, a cop either side of Jess's dad as they took him out to the waiting car.

Jess's mom was screaming and crying and I felt terrible for her and for Jess and their new baby. As her husband disappeared down the steps, Jess's mom sank to the floor, sobbing. And then and there I knew that all of this was my fault.

That poor baby was so new in the world and it needed its mommy and daddy – I wanted to run over there and take the child from her, try and make everything better again, but I couldn't.

Nothing would ever be better for them again.

I had to go to court and give evidence against Jess's dad – it was a very daunting experience. I sat in this little chair with the stenographer on one side of me, typing up everything I said.

But after all that Jess's dad put me through, I didn't feel angry at what he had done. I was still too young to understand what had happened or his motivations. Looking back now of course I feel nothing but disgust for him, but at the time I had no notion that what he had done to me was sexual. It just seemed a very odd thing to do.

And I couldn't understand how the bad thing that he had done to me in his bedroom had caused all this stuff afterwards. It seemed to me that 'telling' made everything so much worse.

In truth I felt sorry for him and his family that he had to go to jail for what he had done to me. Of course, now that I'm an adult I see it all very differently – what he did was appalling and he absolutely deserved to be put in prison. What if Mom hadn't seen me in the bath that night? It could have gone on for months! What if he was abusing others? His own children?

But I was just a child then and I didn't understand what had happened to me. I think some part of me realised this was what grown-ups did together when they were alone in bed, but it didn't strike me as being anything other than a little strange and curious.

From the day she discovered the assault, Mom always checked me down there after I got out of the bath, to make sure I was okay and nobody else was interfering with me.

But by that point it was too late for maternal concern. The wheels were already in motion to take us out of her care.

As soon as she'd reported the molestation to the police, Child Protective Services (CPS) became involved in our lives.

Looking back now it amazes me it took them so long to get interested in us. According to my grandma my brother Mellie had been born with drugs in his system and had to go through detox in the hospital.

It must have been well documented that Mom was a

drug addict but I guess she'd just managed to convince the authorities until this moment that she was working hard to get off the drugs and be a good mother to her kids.

Well now it all started to go wrong.

From the assault at Belport it became apparent Mom was leaving us with unsuitable people in the shelter she barely knew while she was out doing drugs. Jess's dad was a drug-user too.

Mom wasn't deemed fit as a parent until she had her own place and had gone through rehab.

So my brother and sister were packed off to live with my uncle Jerome, his girlfriend Melissa and their five kids while I was allowed to stay with Grandma.

'She loves you more than us!' Momo said spitefully when we were told the news.

It certainly seemed that way – Grandma always welcomed me with open arms. She called me her 'little Munchikin' and in her house I had a room all to myself.

On the first night I was at Grandma's, I asked her why Mellie and Momo couldn't come and live with her too.

But she just shook her head. 'I told her,' she kept repeating, more to herself than me, 'I told her I wasn't going to look after no more of her kids.'

It didn't make sense to me at the time – but there was a lot I didn't understand back then. For one thing, Grandma had already taken on my older brother

Roland. He had been born to my mom when she was 16 and still in school.

Roland was seven years older than me and I didn't think of him as my half-brother – to me, he was like Grandma's kid. But he wasn't – he was my mom Debra's kid and Grandma was doing her best already for all the kids my mom was having and not taking responsibility for.

Of course, I didn't understand any of that at the time. All I knew was that from the moment me, Mellie and Momo were split up, everything changed.

I settled in fine at Grandma's – by now I had started first grade and Grandma made sure I had a good breakfast of oatmeal, milk and sugar every morning before she did my hair.

'Ouch!' I yelped as she pulled the comb through. 'You're hurting me, Grandma!'

'Oh, quit your whining,' she chuckled indulgently. Grandma would never really get mad at me, she never yelled or beat me. Whatever I wanted she gave to me and really I was thoroughly spoilt.

Every morning at 7.30 a.m. Grandma would walk me to the bus stop and see me onto the school bus then she'd wait until the bus had pulled away. One morning I was so mad at her for pulling my hair I stuck my tongue out at her from the top of the bus. I feel bad about that now. Grandma was only doing her best for me and I was probably a rough little child at that point. Life had made me a bit tougher and coarser than I should have been at that age.

On the bus I would be joined by my friends from the block – Keishana, Gordo and Keir. We had fun in class with our lovely teacher Miss Libretto. She was real pretty with long hair, kind blue eyes and she dressed really nice too. One day we built a gingerbread house out of cookies and used icing to cement the sides together. After school we'd ride our bikes up and down the block and play Tag until my grandma called me in for dinner. After dinner I'd play with my Barbies in the Barbie House Grandma bought me or watch TV.

I was happy at my grandma's but I missed Mellie and Momo horribly, especially at night, when I went to sleep all alone. I was so confused about why we'd all been split up.

By this time Mom was going through a really bad patch – at times she would turn up and stay at Grandma's house for a while but then she'd be off for days at a time, and Grandma had no idea where she was or when she was going to turn up again.

Just after lunch one day Mom came storming into the house and started arguing with my grandma, who was sat on her chair in the front room.

I was playing with my doll's house in my room when I heard the commotion from next door. I was filled with mixed emotions: I was pleased Mom was back but I was frightened of her dark moods and unpredictable temper.

'Why don't you just go outside and calm down?' I heard my grandma yelling at her.

'I don't want to go outside!' Mom shouted back. 'I know your game, you old bitch! You're just trying to get rid of me! You're always trying to get rid of me! You just can't stand the sight of me, can you?'

'What are you talking about? Look, I'm not going to sit here and listen to you cussing me out...'

Just then my mom's voice dropped. 'Don't you move a fucking muscle. If you get up out that chair right now, I swear I'll cut your fucking neck off your head.'

I froze, petrified. Then I heard my mom moving to the kitchen.

I heard her muttering to herself, 'Goddamn it! Where are all the goddam knives?'

At that point, with Mom distracted, my grandma flew out of her chair and shoved my mom out of the kitchen onto the front porch and locked the screen door behind her. Now my mom was on the other side of the door screaming at my grandma and I crept up behind her to see what the hell was going on.

As soon as Mom saw me she beckoned for me to come to her: 'Come here, my little Nikki!' she called out to me. 'Come here baby girl!'

I hid behind Grandma's legs. Part of me wanted to go

to my mom but at the same time I knew I couldn't. She was in one of her funny moods again.

Grandma looked at me sternly. 'Now don't you go getting any funny ideas, Nikki. Your mom ain't right today. She can't come in the house.'

I looked around wildly.

Grandpa wasn't in at the time – he was out working. He worked a lot so Grandma was often in the house on her own. Besides, he didn't like to get too involved in family stuff. He was a quiet man and often kept his peace around us, whatever was going on.

Looking at my mom stood outside on the porch, I felt sorry for her and begged my grandma to let her in but she wasn't budging. Instead she went to the phone and called the cops. I'm not sure what happened next or why. The cops came and talked to my grandma and my mom – I think they were just trying to calm everyone down. They didn't take my mom away and, I think, eventually she found refuge at a friend's place nearby. All I know for sure is that I was one confused little girl. All I wanted was to be with my mom but for some reason I couldn't. My heart broke that day.

3
Dad

I DREW IN a deep breath then threw myself head first into the water, kicking my legs and wriggling my body from side to side to get some extra speed. I was challenging myself to see if I could swim a whole length underwater!

My legs flew out wildly behind me but I felt the pressure building up in my lungs and before I could propel myself to the end I came up gasping for air, breaking the surface of the water and reaching out blindly for the edge.

I panted heavily, clinging to the side of the pool and blinking back watery droplets as the summer sun sparkled off the water's surface.

It was Saturday morning so I didn't have school and Grandma had said I could play in the pool in her backyard. As I wiped the water from my face, I saw the door open and Grandma came out with a man I'd never seen before.

He was dressed real nice in a silk shirt and black trousers and had polished black shoes that came clicking towards me at my eye level.

I squinted upwards into the sunlight as the man

squatted down at the pool's edge and my grandma announced: 'Nikki – this is David. He's your dad.'

My dad! *What dad?* Before that moment I had no idea I even had a dad!

All my life I'd grown up calling Beanie Dad so I didn't know there was another man out there who was my real dad.

I looked into the kind, smiling face in front of me and didn't know what to say.

'Hi Nikki,' the man said cheerfully. 'You having a nice time out here in the water?'

I nodded, dumbly. I felt so vulnerable down there in the water, my arms and legs exposed, face dripping wet as he stood there in his smart clothes. I felt embarrassed, stupid even.

I examined this stranger's face – he had pale, slanted eyes, like a cat, and pretty hair too.

Then, his eyebrows shot up and it looked like he'd suddenly been struck with a brainwave: 'Hey, here's a thought. You wanna come over to my house and meet some other kids?'

I looked from him to my grandma, who was grinning encouragingly, so I replied, 'Oh, okay.'

He laughed, seemingly relieved. 'Well, okay. You get out that pool and dry off and I'll take you back to my place to meet your brothers and sister.'

*

After I'd dried off and changed into my jeans and tank top Dad drove me to his house in a place called Amityville, a suburb of New York, about half an hour's drive away.

My mind was whirring all the way there. I've got brothers and a sister? Why didn't anyone tell me? Why didn't anyone tell me about my dad before now?

But I didn't say anything. I was only six years old and this man next to me was a stranger. I'd keep my questions for when I got home to Grandma.

Meeting my brothers and sister for the first time was very strange. David Junior was the eldest; he was nine years old. At seven, my sister Sere was a year older than me and five-year-old Buddy was a year younger than me.

They barely waited until the introductions were over before they started firing questions at me.

'Who do you live with?'

'My grandma.'

'Where's your mom?'

'I don't know.'

'You got other brothers and sisters?'

'Yup.'

'Where they at?'

'With my uncle Jerome.'

'Why aren't they with you?'

'I don't know.'

'Which grade you in?'

'First grade.'

I did my best to answer their questions but it was hard – I didn't always know the answers.

Their mom Theresa seemed kind and after a while she hushed them up and took me through to the kitchen where she offered me ice cream.

We all sat down at the dining table for big bowls of chocolate ice cream and although Sere and Buddy seemed happy I was there, David Junior scowled at me across the table. I got the feeling he didn't like me at all.

It was Sere who seemed nicest. After we had ice cream she took me through to the kids' playroom where she had some really cool toys. One was a pink and white kitchen set and she also liked to play with Barbie dolls, like me.

Afterwards, my dad took us all to Chuck E. Cheese where we played arcade games and in the evening he dropped me back to my grandma's.

'You had fun today?' he asked sweetly as we said goodbye on my grandma's porch.

I nodded, meekly.

'Great! Well, you'll have to come round again next weekend.'

I went straight to sleep that night, too exhausted by the day's unusual turn of events to think or do much.

But the next morning over breakfast I was bursting with questions.

'Why does my dad live with Theresa? Why doesn't he live with my mommy? Why didn't anyone tell me about my dad and my brothers and sister?'

My grandma did her very best but how do you explain to a six-year-old that she's the result of an ill-advised affair?

Much later I learned the truth. Mom had met David when he was still with Theresa. She'd fallen madly in love with him, believing he was the man for her.

But it seems that David didn't feel the same – he already had David Junior and Sere with Theresa and by the time Mom was pregnant with me, the affair had run its course.

David ditched her and shortly afterwards he married Theresa.

Mom was mad, heartbroken and humiliated – she wasn't going to let him get away with it!

So a few weeks after I was born she marched round to Theresa's house while David was out at work and presented me to her love rival.

'This is David's child,' she told her.

Of course Theresa, then pregnant with Buddy, was horrified. She had no idea I existed until that moment. To this day I don't know why Mom did that. Was it to be spiteful? To break up their relationship or maybe just to get David to face up to his responsibilities? Or could it have been during one of her mad, het-up impulsive episodes? I don't think even my mom would know that for sure.

But whatever she thought would be the outcome it didn't work because David stayed with Theresa and Mom went off with Beanie.

But Dad stayed in touch with my grandma and when he heard about the assault on me at Belport he resolved to try and get me back.

I can't imagine how that conversation went with Theresa. How do you cope with taking on your husband's love child? At least she was prepared to try, though it must have been really painful.

That's why David Junior didn't like me. He saw just how hard it was for his mom to welcome me, the evidence of her husband's unfaithfulness, into their home. I guess he must have seen a lot of tears flowing over me and hated me for it. But for what it's worth, Theresa was never anything but kind to me.

For my part, I was just grateful that my dad wanted to be with me and treat me so nice. He started taking me back to their house most weekends and sometimes I'd stay over on Saturday night.

They only had a small, two-bedroom house so my dad and Theresa had one bedroom, the boys another and Sere and I slept on the pull-out couch in the living room. But it was fun, like an adventure.

Every visit Dad arranged special things to do with us, like go to the zoo or the soft play centre and I even got to meet his mom and dad, who were introduced to me as my Nanny and PopPop. They seemed really friendly and had a great big house with bowls laying about the place stuffed with candy.

I didn't mind meeting all these new people. It was a distraction from thinking about my mom, Mellie and Momo. I tried not to think about them all the time but at night, when there was nothing going on, I wondered how they were and worried for my mom. Was she okay?

One day after school I was sprawled out on the couch watching TV when my grandma asked me casually, 'So, you wanna live with your dad?'

I nodded. Why not? It seemed really fun at their house and Grandma said I could come back and see her all the time.

I was six! I didn't understand what it meant to go and live with my dad permanently. I didn't realise that it would mean moving another step away from being reunited with my mom, Mellie and Momo. Up until that point nothing in my life had been permanent.

That weekend it got to midday and I said to my dad, 'Can I go back to Grandma's now please?'

He seemed irritated. 'You know, you're getting ready to live with us so you're not going to be able to say you wanna go back to your grandma's no more. This is going to be your home.'

I just stared at him, confused. I didn't understand – my grandma said I could go back to her anytime. I thought that's what she meant.

*

A few weeks later Grandma came into my room.

'Well, it's decided,' she sad sadly. 'Your dad won custody of you in court today. I guess you better pack up your things.'

'I'm going to go to Dad's now?'

'Yes, my little Munchikin.'

'Can I come back and see you whenever I want?'

'Well, you'll have to ask your dad if you can come over. He's in charge of you now.'

I started to cry. In a way, I wasn't surprised this was happening – it wasn't the first time Mom had left me. But it didn't mean it hurt any less. 'Oh, don't worry little one – everything's going to be fine,' Grandma soothed.

To be honest, I didn't really understand what had happened and why things had worked out this way. I was so young. I don't even know now if Mom had visitation rights. So, I just did what the grown-ups said. I tried not to worry.

I moved in with Dad in October and the following month, 24 November 1997, I turned seven. Dad took us to Chuck E. Cheese again but that was one of the last fun things I remember after moving into his house.

From the moment I left my grandma's house, my dad seemed to change. Out went the indulgent, smiling father who took me on fun trips to the zoo and in came the strict, no-nonsense disciplinarian.

Dad worked as a correctional officer at a local jail and he seemed to bring the same techniques of discipline to bear on his home life.

Suddenly I went from a completely indulged environment, where I never had to lift a finger to help, to one where I was expected to do chores every day. It was a real shock to the system.

We had to make our beds, clean the kitchen, wash the bathroom, take out the trash and do our homework on the kitchen table every night.

If we failed to do our chores properly or our grades slipped, we got put on lockdown!

That meant we had to stay in the kids' room and we weren't allowed out to play or watch TV.

I soon learned to fit in to avoid getting punished and it wasn't long before I became scared of Dad, just like my half-brothers and -sister.

You never knew what mood he was going to be in when he came home at night. Sometimes he seemed really mean and angry and at other times he was sweet as pie. Not knowing who was going to walk in the door was what made him scary.

But no matter how he acted, we always had to give him a hug when he came in or there would be trouble. There were plenty of times I hugged him when I really didn't want to. And every night we had to kiss him goodnight – I hated doing that. It's not like he would kiss you back – he'd just turn his cheek to allow you to plant a kiss and then carry on doing whatever he was doing.

Theresa was kind but Dad was the boss of the house so we couldn't appeal to her to help if we got into trouble. Sometimes he came home really late and although we'd all been up watching TV with Theresa, as soon as we heard his car pull up, we'd run to our own beds and pretend to be asleep, just so we wouldn't have to greet him.

Dad's house was different to anything I'd experienced before – of course at the time I really hated doing those chores but I can't argue with how he raised us. He gave me the tools for adult life: routine, self-discipline and responsibility.

Perhaps that's why Dad didn't like me going over to my grandma's house.

'She spoils you,' he'd say. 'She lets you get away with anything.'

And it was true. At Grandma's house I didn't have to do a damn thing! Even if she asked me to do something and I didn't do it, I never got told off. And I could get away with acting really bad with Grandma – she never raised her voice to me. It didn't matter if I acted up, if I didn't listen or I lied, I could get away with it. There were no consequences at Grandma's house.

Dad may not have liked me going to my grandma's but at least he allowed it because he recognised my grandma looked after me properly. When it came to my mom, that was a different matter altogether.

My dad didn't want me to see my mom at all!

When I was with my mom, we were either left to do whatever we wanted or I was saddled with all the responsibility of a grown-up, being in charge of two kids.

I know he was only looking out for me, doing his best to keep me from what he saw as a neglectful parent, but she was my mom and I loved her. I missed her so much. Before he'd shown up in my life she was the only parent I'd known.

So at the weekend, Grandma would pick me up and Mom would come round to Grandma's with Mellie and Momo. The first time I saw them, I squeezed them so tight. It was like I felt complete again.

That's how we managed to get round Dad's rules.

One weekend in November, shortly after my birthday, I was over at Grandma's house with my mom, Momo and Mellie when my mom started moaning with pain. I didn't know what was going on except Grandma suddenly got quite agitated. She was trying to get us kids off to bed while my mom rested up in the lounge.

As usual, Momo and I were jumping on the beds but this time, instead of indulging us as she usually did, my grandma got angry with us.

'Come on now, you two,' she admonished. 'That's enough. Don't you think I got enough to be doing without you pair foolin' about like that?'

Later that night we heard Mom's screams and later still my grandpa's truck pulled out of the driveway.

The next morning Grandma told us all what had happened. 'You've got a new baby brother. His name is Hasson but your mom says we're gonna call him Sonny for short.'

I was so excited! A baby – I loved babies!

Later that evening Mom came back home with the baby and she even let me hold him. Oh he was so beautiful – I didn't want to leave him.

'Now don't you go telling your dad I've had a baby,' Mom warned me. 'That's not something he's gonna want to know.'

'I won't,' I promised solemnly.

But I was so excited about the baby, I couldn't keep it to myself. As soon as I got back to Dad's house that night I blurted out: 'I have something to tell you but I'm not supposed to. My mom had a baby! He's called Sonny and he's really cute. She let me hold him. I love him so much. Can I go back again soon, Dad? Please?'

Dad and Theresa looked at each other meaningfully. By now Mom had five children with four different fathers.

It's true that I loved babies but it seemed that Mom

loved them even more! At the time, I was so young it didn't strike me as strange that Mom was allowed to keep Sonny, but not me and my brother and sister.

But then, not long after Sonny was born, Mom got her own apartment, round the corner from us in Amityville at 501 Broadway, and Mellie and Momo went back to live with her.

Dad still didn't like me going to see her so Grandma would pick me up from his house at the weekend and she'd drop me round at Mom's.

I loved holding the baby and feeding him and Mom seemed happy to let me look after him. In fact, she left me in charge of Mellie, Momo and the baby sometimes! I was still only seven.

It wasn't always easy – one time I was sat on the bed trying to feed Sonny while Mom was sleeping and I dropped him onto the stone fireplace next to the bed!

Oh my God, my heart nearly stopped. I thought I'd killed my baby brother!

I nearly cried with happiness when he started screaming but then I was gripped with fear – what if I'd injured him for life? What if he'd hit his head and he wound up in hospital?

I was petrified.

Mom woke up with a start when she heard the baby crying and quickly grabbed him off me.

'What happened?' she demanded angrily.

'He fell,' I whispered quietly. 'I was holding him. I was

trying to feed him but he slipped and fell. I'm sorry, Mommy.'

'You stupid little girl!' she snapped at me. 'This is a baby – a real live baby! Not a dumb doll! You can't drop babies! Why didn't you rest him on the bed while you were getting him his bottle? You've got to think!

'How can I trust you to look after this child if you're going to treat him no better than one of your dolls! You think I can trust you again now to hold him?'

I started crying but she ignored my tears and kept rocking him till he was soothed and quietened down.

That night I cried myself to sleep. I was doing my best but I was only small myself and my arms weren't big enough to hold Sonny and feed him at the same time. Looking back, I can't believe I was left in charge, but at the time I felt like the worst person in the world. I'd been so proud to be treated like a grown-up and I'd got it all wrong.

I suppose Mom did find it in her heart to trust me with the baby because soon after that she was happy to leave me in charge of him again.

One time she just put him next to me when I was asleep on the bed.

I woke up to the sound of his cries to find that he'd rolled off the side of the bed against a wall and was lying directly on the heater!

Poor thing – his little face was squashed between the mattress and the wall.

I picked him up – he felt really hot! How long had he been there?

Fortunately he stopped crying after a few minutes and I guess he was okay but what if I hadn't woken up? He could have stayed on that heater all night long.

I took him into the living room where Mom was entertaining her friends as usual and put him back in her arms without saying a word, then took myself back off to bed.

On the whole I liked visiting Mom – her house was on a really busy road but once you went through the front gate the grass on her lawn went all the way round her house and me, Mellie and Momo loved to play out there in the day.

One time Mom took us outside and played tea parties with the dolls and the teacups. She even made us frozen juices in little cups.

From the front porch steps up to the house the kitchen area was immediately in front of you and if you turned right there was the living room with the fireplace in it.

Mom sometimes slept on the pull-out couch in the living room.

I remember the house was really dark – the walls and floor seemed to be made of dark wood.

There were two bedrooms and me, Mellie and Momo usually slept in our red bunk beds in one of the bedrooms.

But you couldn't rely on Mom – even if we'd had a good day together, by the evening she would usually end up acting strange.

She used to stand at the window at the front and cross herself over and over again. Or she'd walk round the house, reciting the Lord's Prayer out loud.

She still had lots of friends that came and went from the house, maybe more this time because Amityville wasn't the greatest area. Even at seven years old I could tell that Mom lived in a really run-down part of the city. There were loads of crackheads just walking round the streets and they'd always come and ask you for money, no matter if you were just seven like me! They were always real skinny and small and some of them acted jittery and their teeth chattered. Those were the ones you had to avoid – the ones who were wired, who really wanted to get a hit.

I never got robbed but I know lots of people that did.

I could tell a crackhead from 100 yards away, just from the way they walked and the fast, furious manner they had about them, so I just crossed the road to avoid them.

How did I know they were wired? Because I'd seen Mom like that plenty of times – real jittery and anxious, like she couldn't wait another minute longer for something and her legs shaking like crazy.

But Grandma told me Mom was doing really well and I guess it looked like she was. She had her own apartment again, she had Mellie and Momo back and soon we were going to have a big party to celebrate!

4
Birthday Party

'YOU CAN'T CATCH me!' I yelled from the backyard as Momo came careering out of the house and round the side of the pool, her little legs pumping like crazy.

Behind her Mellie struggled to keep up, scampering in her wake.

I dodged around the pool as Momo made a grab for me then hopped off the decking and double-backed on myself to race towards the house.

But just at that moment my cousin Shany, Jerome's daughter, came bowling out of the back door, catching me by my collar and swinging me round till we both ended up spinning into the dirt in the backyard and lying on the floor in a heap.

'IT!' she screeched into my ear. 'You're IT! I got you!'

Momo by now had turned back towards where me and Shany lay on the ground and threw herself head first onto our pile of limbs.

Soon Mellie too had joined us by belly-flopping onto our heap, giggling at the silliness of it all.

At that moment I saw my grandma appear in the doorway, a shadow of disapproval crossing her face.

'Now you kids – don't be getting your nice clothes all mussed up! I ain't changing none of you now you're all in your good clothes.'

We all scrambled to our feet and I made an effort to pat the dirt off my dress – I didn't want to get dirty wearing my special party dress.

It was the nicest outfit I'd ever had – a lilac silk dress with blue flowers that just skimmed the top of my knees and short sleeves.

Grandma bought me one and she also bought one in green for Shany, who was three months older than me, so we looked like twins!

I loved my lilac dress but that day Shany's mom Melissa had put a matching green headband in Shany's hair so I felt a little jealous.

Grandma had done my hair earlier that day, unbraiding my plaits, washing my hair then replaiting it, but she didn't have any lilac headbands so I just had in a red clip at the side.

'It don't go with my dress,' I complained petulantly to my grandma as she yanked my wild hair back into plaits.

'You look beautiful, honey,' Grandma soothed. 'Just you be thankful you've got a nice pretty grown-up dress and quit your whining.'

It's true, my dress was beautiful. I don't remember ever owning something quite so lovely and silky. I adored the way it felt on my skin and looked so smart. Looking back now, I'm sure it was polyester but at the moment I didn't care – it was my special party dress and I felt really pretty in it. That's all I knew.

It was Saturday 14 June – the big party day.

Mellie's fifth birthday fell on 9 June and Momo's sixth was just three days later on 12 June, so two days later Grandma held a big birthday party for all us kids at her house in Coconut Street.

There was a large crowd of us that day – me, Mellie and Momo, Mom, Grandma, Grandpa, my uncle Jerome, his girlfriend Melissa and their five kids.

Dad had let me stay over for the weekend so I'd spent the night before in my bed at Grandma's and on Saturday the other kids came over and we hung round the pool while the adults got the party ready.

Grandma made all our favourite foods – fried chicken with collard greens and macaroni cheese – hung up balloons and streamers and played loud reggae music.

She'd even got us all special party outfits – my brother was dressed the same as his cousin in white shirts with navy sleeves and matching navy trousers, Shany and I were wearing our special dresses and my sister was wearing a green dress with white polka dots, just like her cousin who was also six.

The six of us looked like three sets of twins but we didn't mind one bit. It was great of my grandma to make such an effort to put on a big party for us.

All day long we'd been indulged with packets of naughty party food like chips and cheese puffs and we knocked ourselves out with long, energetic games of Tag, Hide and Go Seek and It. It felt wonderful to be hanging out with my family again.

I'd felt the strain of the last few months quite badly. I tried to fit in with all the rules and routines of my new family but the constant ache of longing for my true family didn't make it any easier.

I tried to be on my best behaviour, but it wasn't always easy.

I liked Sere but David Junior wasn't very nice to me and we got into a few scraps. I guess I didn't like to be teased so when he called me stupid I didn't stand for it. One time he hit me in the stomach but I just punched him straight back. Of course we both got into trouble and we were put on punishment for a week.

In the beginning I really hadn't understood that I was living with my dad full-time – I thought eventually I would be allowed to go back to my grandma's and live with her. But as the weeks turned into months it dawned on me that I wasn't ever going to be allowed back with her and that I would just have to be content with my weekend visits.

It was confusing to suddenly be denied all the things I loved and was used to in my life, like seeing my grandma and my brother and sister.

I could tell Dad didn't approve of me coming to see my family and that made it difficult to ask him if I could go over. What if he said no? I was afraid of being disappointed, and I resented him for making it so difficult to see my own family, which I thought was my natural right!

When I was at my grandma's I was free and I could relax and be myself. Grandma had known me all my life and I was comfortable around her. Just pulling up into her drive, I felt like I breathed a little easier. As she walked out of the house to greet me I'd throw myself headlong into her arms and hang on to her with all my might.

I guess that can't have been easy for my dad to see – maybe that's why he disliked me going round to my grandma's so much.

After my weekends away he'd grumble: 'Of course you love her – she gives you everything you want. Who wouldn't want that? But no one ever said that was right for a child.'

Today was extra special though. For the first time in ages all us kids were together.

Here in Grandma's backyard, running around with my brother, sister and all my cousins again, I felt like I was back where I belonged. I screamed, laughed, poked, jumped, joked and teased to my heart's content.

Here I was the older one, the bossyboots, the big girl. Although Shany was three months older than me, she wasn't as streetwise or smart-mouthed as me so I was the one in charge. This was my territory – I wasn't in someone else's house, creeping round, trying not to upset anyone, trying not to annoy the older brother who didn't like me anyway.

It felt good being the big girl again but without all the responsibilities of looking out for the younger ones, like I had when I was at my mom's place.

Here, there were grown-ups to do the grown-up things like looking after the baby and nobody locked us out!

Eventually at around 4 p.m. my grandma called us all in to the basement where Momo and Mellie were given their presents.

I tried not to be jealous when I saw Momo ripping the shiny paper from her gifts. She got two beautiful dolls and a brilliant Crayola craft set to make badges while Mellie got three new toy cars.

Meanwhile Mom was hopping around with her camera, excitedly snapping the magical moments of surprise that would light up Momo and Mellie's faces as each of them unwrapped their presents.

I liked the look of the Crayola craft set. While Momo was busy with her dolls, I picked it up and opened up the lid. Inside there were special stickers to colour in, magic markers and glitter sticks to decorate the badges.

It looked so cool.

Just then Momo turned round.

'Hey!' she barked, making a grab for the box. 'That's mine! It's not for you.'

'Chill out,' I said. 'I'm only looking at it. I'm not going to do anything.'

'I want to look at it first,' said Momo sulkily. 'You shouldn't be opening the box. It's my birthday present, not yours.'

'Come on now,' my mom soothed. 'Nikki, honey, why don't you give the craft set back to Momo cos it is her present after all and she should look at it first.'

'Sure,' I said, feigning indifference. 'I don't care.'

Mom knelt down in front of us both as Momo snatched the box possessively from my hands and wrapped her arms round it.

'There you go, you two. Why don't you hug and make up and I'll take a picture? You two look real cute in your party dresses.'

But Momo was still in a mood. She pouted obstinately at the camera and pointedly inched away from me on the sofa.

'No – I don't want to give her a hug,' she puffed. 'She tried to steal my present. She tried to open the box up.'

'No I didn't,' I said, quick to defend myself. 'I wasn't stealing it! I was just looking.'

But Momo continued pouting angrily in my direction.

'There – what a beautiful face,' Mom joked, snapping a picture of Momo's angry scowl. 'What a stunning, pretty little girl you are today! My goodness, Momo, you should be a model!'

Momo couldn't resist my mom's gentle teasing and no matter how hard she tried to keep that pout on, her lips started to curl up in the corners of her mouth and when my mom grabbed her to tickle her the smile turned into shrieking laughter.

She wriggled out of Mom's arms and slunk under the table to escape.

'And you're not getting away without a tickle too!' Mom shouted, lunging at me. I screamed and ran round the side of the settee.

Then I let her grab me and throw me up in the air. At that moment I was so happy and free, I felt I could fly away.

'Hat-time everyone!' Grandma shouted, appearing from the kitchen with silver foil pointy party hats.

She handed them all out and then Mom got up and dimmed the lights while Aunt Melissa appeared at the door carefully balancing a cake ablaze with candles, and everyone started up singing 'Happy Birthday' to Mellie and Momo.

I looked over at my mom – she was radiant, her

cheeks glowing with happiness. It was lovely, us all being together like this.

After we finished singing Mellie and Momo took in two massive breaths and blew their candles out.

We all crowded in next to them to get a better look at the cake. There was Bugs Bunny, Daffy Duck, Elmer Fudd and Tweetie Pie, all wishing Mellie and Momo Happy Birthday!

'Say "cheese" everyone!' Mom sang cheerily, as she crouched in front of us.

We all grinned, anticipating the cake being cut and everyone getting a large slice.

The camera clicked, capturing our eager, shiny young faces for ever, locking us up together in a moment of true childhood happiness – me, Momo and Mellie.

Snap!

I still have this picture today and I look at it often.

If I could pick one moment in time I'd like to return to, it's this one. My grandma's basement, dinnertime, Saturday 14 June 1998.

It's the last time I remember being truly happy.

5

Brooklyn

I WAS OUT in the front yard when I spied the truck rolling slowly down our street.

It was late afternoon on Saturday 20 June, a week after the birthday party. I was at my dad's place and was picking dandelions with Sere, Buddy and David Junior. We'd each gathered a small handful to take back inside when my grandpa's familiar red truck pulled up next to the house.

I straightened up, an excited grin spreading across my face – was my grandma coming to get me for the weekend? What a great surprise!

But my smile quickly faded as I made out my grandma's worried look behind the wheel and Mom's strange, fixed stare. In the back of the truck Mellie and Momo were sat on the bare floor, and Momo was holding Sonny who was screaming his head off.

This didn't look right.

As soon as Mom got out of the cab I could tell she was in one of her moods. And what were those blue marks up and down her arms and legs? I squinted to get a better look. Was it writing?

She strode towards me in her red shirt, jean shorts and sneakers. By now the other kids had stopped picking flowers too and they were staring at my mom as she walked purposefully towards us.

As she got nearer I could make out what she had written on her limbs. She'd scrawled her name over and over again up and down her arms and legs: Debra Roberson, Debra Roberson, Debra Roberson, the repetition only occasionally broken up with the odd cross she'd drawn on herself.

Sere inched closer to me and whispered in my ear. 'What's wrong with your mom?'

I couldn't answer – I didn't know.

I looked behind my mom to Grandma, who was just staring straight ahead – she looked really stressed out.

Just then Mom burst through the front gate and grabbed my arm. Too stunned to even greet her I blurted out: 'Mom, why did you write your name on yourself?'

But it was like she couldn't hear me and she didn't answer.

'Mom?' I said anxiously. 'Mom?'

'Come on,' she said. 'We have to go.' And with that she started pulling me towards the truck.

But I resisted, digging my heels into the grass and leaning back against the weight of her body.

'No, wait, Mom!' I told her. 'I gotta go inside and tell Theresa where I'm going.'

But Mom just yanked harder on my arm and I stumbled towards her.

'No, you don't,' she replied and just kept dragging me towards the red truck. Meanwhile Sonny was screaming and David, Buddy and Sere were too stunned to move.

As she dragged me out of the gate and towards the truck, I felt panic rising.

'Mom, wait, *please*!' I implored desperately. 'I have to tell Daddy and Theresa where I'm going or I'll get into trouble.'

But the conversation was over.

She picked me up and put me in the back of the truck next to my sister, who was struggling to hold Sonny.

Then Mom got in the front next to Grandma, who had the engine running, and we drove off.

As we pulled away down the street I saw Sere suddenly spring to life, running inside the house, calling for her mom.

Buddy was still just standing there in the front yard, his mouth open in shock, a scattering of forgotten dandelions at his feet.

And that was that – I guess my mom had suddenly decided that she didn't want to wait any longer to see me so she just kidnapped me instead.

I was pleased to see my family of course but it was disturbing to see Mom looking so crazy and my brother and sister so upset.

Mellie was quiet and took my hand for reassurance, while Momo scowled at me as she jiggled Sonny up and down. From her look I could tell Mom had been like this all day.

It didn't take long to get back to Grandma's house and within a short time, Mom had calmed down. Grandma got all us kids inside and bustled about the kitchen, whipping up a tuna casserole for dinner.

Momo handed me Sonny and stomped off to watch TV and I sat down on the sofa to feed the baby, who by now had stopped crying.

What had happened here today? I wondered.

Mom's moods were so unreliable – she'd seemed so happy last week but now she'd slipped away again.

'Don't worry, honey-pie,' Grandma said as she caught sight of my worried expression. 'I'll call your dad and let him know you're here with me this weekend. You won't get into trouble. Your mom wanted to see you real bad today and well, I guess we all wanted to see you!'

She smiled reassuringly but I could still see the concern in her eyes. I think at times Grandma found it difficult to say no to my mom. And, when she was in one of her moods it was usually just easier to placate her.

I nodded, relieved someone else would be telling my dad what had happened, but looking across the room, I could see my mom standing by the window crossing herself and mumbling something incomprehensible.

She was lost in another world.

This wasn't the mom I'd played with at the birthday party the week before – this was the other mom, the one who acted crazy, who wrote on herself and did strange things. As I got ready for bed that night, I hoped that by the next morning, my real mom would be back.

Waking up the next day, curled up next to Momo on one side and Mellie on the other, I gave a little wriggle of happiness. This is what I loved the best – being warm and safe in the comforting surroundings of Coconut Street surrounded by my family.

I lay there for a second, just enjoying the peace and quiet of the early morning, the familiar sounds of my grandma in the kitchen and the warmth of our three bodies under the blankets.

Then I turned over to see that Momo's eyes were wide open and she gave me a playful poke. I poked her back and we both giggled. Then we gently eased ourselves off the bunk bed, leaving Mellie to sleep a little longer. My heart swelled with joy. At last, I felt at home with my little brother and sister, my best friends.

We crept out of the room in our pyjamas to see my grandma at the sink, elbow-deep in washing-up.

'Well, good morning, sleepyheads!' she exclaimed, coming over to give us each a big, soapy hug. 'How's about some Fruit Loops then?'

We both nodded and while Grandma made herself busy, bringing out the bowls, spoons, cereal and milk, we flicked on the TV to watch *Rugrats*.

Later on, she came over and asked: 'How do you fancy going to Brooklyn today? Seeing your uncle Alma and your cousins?'

'Sure,' we both garbled through mouthfuls of sugary cereal.

I loved going to Brooklyn where Grandma's brother Alma lived with his family. Grandma had lots of brothers and sisters but Alma had three kids our age and we all got on really well. Their apartment was really big, overlooking a playground and a basketball court where there were always tonnes of other kids hanging round to have fun with.

The rest of the morning me, Mellie and Momo messed about, watched TV and looked after Sonny while Grandma and my mom got ready for our outing.

Outside, it was cold and overcast so Mom had on long jeans and a black shirt, covering up the writing on her arms and legs. Now that the home-made tattoos that she'd drawn with pen were hidden, I almost forgot Mom's strange behaviour yesterday.

In the middle of the afternoon, we loaded ourselves into the car – me, Momo, Mellie, Sonny and my mom and Grandma, who drove.

Alma's house was in Brooklyn, which was a long way from Coconut Street in Brentwood. Grandpa was busy on a call-out from his work so this time we went in Grandma's car, a red Chevy Oldsmobile.

Everything seemed fine at first but in the 45 minutes it took us to get to Brooklyn, the sky darkened, and with it Mom's mood.

We pulled up to the apartment just as the first drops of rain were beginning to fall and Grandma hurried to get us inside the apartment on the third floor. But by now Mom didn't want to go inside.

She looked mean and angry.

'These kids are staying with me,' she told Grandma. 'You go in – we'll be in later.'

She was holding my wrist tight, almost hurting me, and had my baby brother in the crook of her other arm.

My grandma just shrugged and went inside, calling back to us over her shoulder, 'Don't be too long. It looks like there's a big old storm coming soon and you don't want them children getting wet.'

Me, Momo and Mellie watched her small body disappear inside the apartment then Mom led us round to the park.

By now the rain was spattering steadily on our heads and thin summer shirts but Mom didn't seem to notice.

Still gripping my wrist she ordered Mellie to hold my other hand and Momo to hold his hand so we were all in a line.

As we walked into the park behind the apartment

building a young girl with another baby stopped to admire Sonny in Mom's arms.

'Ah, he's adorable...' she began, with a smile, but at that moment Mom exploded.

'DON'T YOU TALK TO HIM!' she screamed in her face.

The startled young girl jumped back in shock.

'HE'S JUST A BABY!' Mom shouted, eyes bulging and face contorted with anger. 'HE'S A LITTLE BABY, YOU HEAR? HE AIN'T GOING TO HAVE NO GIRL-FRIEND!'

The girl looked frightened. Clasping her own child closer to her body, she hurried away, clearly freaked out by my mom's strange outburst.

We were all frightened but we didn't know what to do or say – from past experiences we knew that whatever we said could make her worse. Mom threw her head back to stare up to the sky, her eyes ablaze with an inner fire.

What's going on? I thought nervously. Where's Grandma? Where's Uncle Alma?

I scanned the park, the playground and the apartment blocks behind us but I couldn't see anyone I recognised.

I prayed Grandma or Uncle Alma would appear soon and take us inside the apartment but nobody had come out after us.

Momo looked scared too – the sudden outburst made her recoil, dropping Mellie's hand. She backed slowly away, as if heading to Uncle Alma's apartment.

'COME BACK HERE!' Mom screamed at her. 'DON'T YOU TAKE ANOTHER STEP! YOU HEAR ME, MISSY? OR THERE'LL BE TROUBLE AND YOU'LL GET A WHOOPING YOU AIN'T NEVER GONNA FORGET!'

Momo stopped in her tracks and reluctantly came back to the line, picking up Mellie's hand. Tears were welling up in her eyes but she pushed up her chin, too stubborn and proud to cry in front of Mom.

Mom led us towards a bench in front of the playground in the park. People were moving out of our way, wary of the manic, screaming woman and her bedraggled collection of wet children.

I wanted to ask for help but I didn't know what to say and I was scared of getting into trouble. Instead, after we sat down on the bench I asked Mom: 'Can we go and play?'

It was the only way I could think to get us away from her.

'NO!' she yelled, her crazed eyes boring into me. 'You can't play. You can only PRAY! You have to pray for your souls or the devil is going to get you. Yes, and he's going to possess you completely and you'll be sent to hell forever. Now get down on your knees and pray, goddammit! PRAY! PRAY!!'

So we all got on our knees on the wet ground, put our hands together and started reciting the Lord's Prayer.

'Our Father, who art in Heaven, Hallowed be thy

name. Thy kingdom come, thy will be done, On earth, as it is in heaven…'

Mom's voice came ringing over the top of ours: 'Louder. Louder! I can't hear you!'

We raised our voices: 'GIVE US THIS DAY OUR DAILY BREAD…'

Mom now turned her face up towards heaven, shouting: 'Lord, listen to these children. Listen to their prayers. The devil is inside them. Save them from the devil!'

With my head bowed, I stole a glance to where my mom was still sat on the bench above us and I could see she was trying to hold Sonny's hands together in supplication.

'…AND FORGIVE US OUR TRESPASSES, AS WE FORGIVE THOSE WHO TRESPASS AGAINST…'

'Oh Lord!' she cried out, her voice breaking with angry tears. 'Take the devil away from us. Take him away!'

By now we were shouting through the rain, which was coming down in sheets, drenching us to the skin and making us all shiver.

Mothers and their children, teenagers with bikes, dog walkers and skateboarders all huddled under trees to escape the downpour.

Some openly stared but most looked away, embarrassed by the bizarre scene, unable or unwilling to get involved.

'AND LEAD US NOT INTO TEMPTATION BUT DELIVER US FROM EVIL. FOR THINE IS THE KINGDOM, THE POWER AND THE GLORY, FOR EVER AND EVER. AMEN.'

Me and Momo looked sideways at one another and then slowly, fearfully lifted our heads. Mom had Sonny's hands together in prayer and her eyes closed, seemingly swept up in the moment of divinity and exaltation.

My knees were now sore so I put my hands down on the ground to push myself onto my feet and that's when Mom's eyes flipped open and her head swivelled towards me.

'STAY WHERE YOU ARE!' she ordered, her body shaking with fevered anger. 'AGAIN! Say your prayers again. You gotta save your goddamn souls from the devil because he's coming for you, Nikki. He wants to poison your soul and damn you to eternal hell.'

Reluctantly we put our hands together and started up again: 'Our Father, who art in Heaven...'

On and on it went as the rain poured down on us – I wanted to cry.

Where was my grandma? Where was anybody?

By now I didn't care who came and got us – it could have been a stranger – I just wanted to get away from Mom.

Eventually, she let us get up and after about an hour, I was relieved to see Grandma coming towards us holding an umbrella.

'What are you still doing out here? Get these children inside now or they'll all catch their deaths,' she admonished, taking Sonny out of my mom's arms. He was wet through and screaming his head off.

At first it looked like Grandma's appearance had succeeded in calming Mom down. She stopped screaming and praying and Grandma ushered us all back to the apartment while Mom walked silently behind us.

But as we got into the apartment complex, Mom switched again and we heard the angry outburst erupt behind us.

'What the FUCK are you staring at!' she exploded at the curious folk hanging out their windows. Then she started banging on doors and swearing. 'What the fuck you all looking at? What do you want? Heathen! Devil's spawn! Get back behind me, Satan – take your evil away from me!'

Grandma quickened the pace and we all moved up the stairs towards the apartment, Mom banging, cursing and crashing behind us.

We were now in the corridor on the third floor and close to the apartment, all of us practically running.

Then Mom made a grab for my arm.

'I'm not going in that unholy place,' she shrieked. 'And these children ain't going in there neither. That apartment is possessed. It's possessed by the devil. I can feel it. I can feel Satan's hot hellish breath in there, Momma.

'You ain't gonna make me go in there. I'm taking the children back home right now. Right this minute. We all gonna get back on the subway and go home where we'll be safe.'

Alarmed, my grandma handed Sonny to Momo and made a grab for my other arm.

'Well you're not taking Nikki!' she yelled back at my mom. 'You can take the other children but you can't take Nikki. She's here under my care and if anything happens to her I'll get in trouble. Take the others but you can't take Nikki!'

Mom yanked on my arm so hard I flew towards her. 'I'm taking my daughter!'

But Grandma wasn't letting go and I felt my shoulders ache with the strain as she held firm.

'NO!' she said again to my mom. 'David has custody of her and I'm supposed to be watching her right now.'

But Mom just kept going on. 'I'm taking my daughter, I'm taking her, I'm taking her.'

They fought over me, dragging me first one way then the other as hot tears rolled silently down my cheeks.

By now Alma and some of the rest of the family, who must have heard the commotion outside the flats, had come out to see what was going on. As Mom and Grandma fought their tug-of-war over me, my aunt quietly ushered Momo, Mellie and Sonny inside.

What is happening? I screamed inwardly for the hundredth time that day.

I was used to Mom's funny moods but this was horrible. I just wanted everything to stop.

Eventually Grandma must have got through to Mom because she let go of my arm and Grandma took me inside, leaving the door open behind her.

From that moment my uncle and his family enveloped me in their warmth and love, fussing about us kids to get us out of our wet clothes and into some dry ones. I let myself go limp as my aunt towel-dried my hair and my cousins picked out some of their clothes for me, slowly letting the heat seep back into my wet, frozen bones.

Eventually, Mom calmed down enough to come inside and all us kids disappeared into my cousins' room. Unable to process or understand what had just happened, we tried to block out the trauma of the past hour and instead concentrated on playing with my cousins' dolls and cars.

Mom had spent all her energy on her earlier outbursts and now she was just sat in a corner, clasping her Bible and quietly reciting psalms and prayers to herself under her breath.

My aunt made us a delicious dinner of fried chicken and mashed potatoes and when it began to get dark we got back in Grandma's car for the ride back to Long Island.

It was late by the time we returned to Amityville and

Momo, Mellie and Sonny were asleep. I watched them lying there, so peaceful. I hoped that in their dreams they had gone to a good place, somewhere lovely, to make up for the terror of that day. As Mom and Grandma carried them into the house one by one, I wished that I could be with them too. Perhaps we could whisper in the dark about what had happened that day, work out what it was that made our mom so crazy wild. Perhaps we didn't even need to say anything, just being together, being there for each other, would be enough. But that wasn't our life at the moment. We could only see each other when the grown-ups allowed.

Before Grandma drove off, Mom came down and kissed me on the forehead, stroking my face and smiling into my eyes. There was an intensity to her gaze that worried and frightened me, but I couldn't put into words what it was. So I let her kiss me, and say goodbye, and head up to the apartment where my brothers and sister were sleeping.

Grandma dropped me back at my dad's house. I didn't want to go back but Grandma insisted. I had school the next morning after all.

6

The Day Everything Changed

'Hey – we're home!' Buddy called as we all stomped in the house after school.

As usual we slammed our backpacks down in the front porch then ran through to the kitchen to grab a snack.

Theresa was stood at the window, talking quietly into the cordless phone, her hand cupped over the receiver. She quickly looked up as David Junior opened the fridge door. I caught a strange, scared look on her face, her eyes red and puffy.

'Grab us a soda!' Sere called to him.

'Yeah, me too!' I echoed, picking out a packet of chips from the cupboard.

'Hey Mom!' Sere yelled excitedly, tugging on her skirt. 'Is Dad home? Why's his car in the driveway?'

It was only 3 p.m. when we got in from school and Dad didn't usually get back till at least gone eight o'clock every night, so we were surprised to see his car in the drive. After all, it was Thursday 26 June, just a normal day.

Theresa waved Sere away then turned her back to us and went on whispering into the receiver. Any minute we expected her to put her hand to the phone and give us all hell, telling us all to quieten down or at least not to take too many snacks before dinner. But she barely paid us any mind.

So I pulled out three more packs of chips and, loaded up with refreshments, we all headed into the living room.

'Why's Dad's car here?' Buddy repeated as we kicked off our shoes and inched off our jackets.

'Beats me!' said David Junior dismissively.

'Maybe he's got a day off?' Sere offered as we started tearing open packs of chips and unpicking the tops of our soda cans.

I plonked myself down on the sofa and David turned on the TV. This is what we were all looking forward to after a long day in school – relaxing in front of the TV with some snacks. But no sooner had we switched it on than Theresa came bowling out of the kitchen.

'Get that TV off!' she shrieked, the phone dangling in her hand.

'Why?' said David.

'Because I said so – now turn it off, will you!'

None of us moved – I'd never seen Theresa like this before. She was acting really jumpy and strange.

I looked over to Sere who looked equally perplexed.

'We just wanna watch some cartoons before we do

our homework, Ma,' she pleaded. 'What's wrong with that? We always watch cartoons.'

'I said "Off!" Now! Do what I say, missy, or I'll get your father in this minute.'

That was it. Buddy jumped up from the sofa and turned it off. None of us wanted to get into trouble with Dad, even if we didn't understand what we'd done wrong.

'You can do your homework first,' Theresa went on. 'And then you can go play outside.'

'That's not fair!' David railed but Theresa had already disappeared down the corridor and into the main bedroom.

We all looked at each other blankly. What the hell was going on?

Sere and I crept forwards towards Theresa and Dad's bedroom. From the crack of the doorway hinge, I could see our dad was lying down on the bed. Theresa was sitting next to him, her hand resting on his chest.

I could just make out their voices.

'Well, I think we better do it together then...' Theresa was saying.

'You think she'll be okay?'

'Who knows? We just gotta be here for her... Poor thing.'

What was going on? It didn't look or sound good. Maybe we were in trouble. I tried to rack my brains to think of everything I'd done that morning. Had I cleaned up after myself at breakfast? Did I make my bed?

I thought everything was fine but looking back now I couldn't be sure – maybe I'd forgotten something. Was it my turn to take out the trash?

'You think we're in trouble?' I whispered nervously to Sere.

'I don't know,' she replied, her eyes wide with confusion. 'I hope not but I don't know. This is definitely not normal.'

We tiptoed back to the living room and rescued our workbooks from our backpacks in the front porch, then stretched out on the floor to do our homework.

A short time later, Theresa appeared in the doorway.

'Nikki, honey,' she said softly. 'Why don't you come with me?'

I reluctantly got up – I didn't know what was going on but I didn't like the sound of it. Theresa was smiling at me but her eyes were still puffy and she looked like she'd been crying.

She led me into the bedroom where my dad was lying down on the bed – as I came in, he pushed himself up to sitting. Dad didn't look right either – his face looked all funny and his voice was real soft.

'Nikki – come sit down next to me,' he said, patting his purple silky bedspread.

I didn't like this at all. I started to get a funny feeling

in the pit of my stomach. Why was he smiling at me? A smile that only reached to the top of his lips and no further. Why was I the only one in there?

I looked back at Theresa who was standing next to me.

'We have to talk to you,' she added. 'Please. Sit down.'

This felt wrong – I wanted to run out of there and get on my bike and ride away. Whatever they had to say to me, it didn't feel like it was going to be good. But I didn't run – I sat down, right where Dad had patted a space. My whole body was tense, nervous as hell.

Dad took a long time before he said anything again. I kept looking at him then back up to Theresa who was staring intensely at my dad.

He had his eyes cast down at the bedspread, then he sighed heavily. Finally he looked up at me and, really, really slowly, he said: 'Nikki. You're not going to see your brother and sister any more. You can't – because Mellie and Momo passed away.'

I felt a huge sob rising inside me. I knew what passed away meant. It meant dead. My brother and sister were dead. I knew the words but I couldn't understand it.

I'd only seen them a few days ago!

I looked from my dad to Theresa, in shock. This couldn't be true. How could it be true?

'What happened?' I managed to get out as the tears started to fall.

My dad took me in his arms and rocked me as I sobbed and sobbed. I felt his chest rising and falling too.

'They're gone,' was all he'd say. 'They're just gone, Nikki.'

There are no words for what I was feeling. It was as if somebody had reached into the deepest part of me and ripped out my insides. Mellie and Momo meant everything to me. I'd loved and protected them both since they were babies. I'd played with them and prayed with them. We'd stuck together through everything, our hearts beating together through pain and happiness.

How could they be dead?

My dad held me for ages but I couldn't stop the tears from coming. In truth, I didn't want to be held by him, I just wanted to curl up next to Mellie and Momo like I always did. Cuddle them close next to me. My body ached to hold them both in my arms.

After a while my dad got up and, cradling me still in his arms, he placed me in the leather recliner in their room. I heard him and Theresa whispering above me but it was like I couldn't see or feel anything apart from the terrible pain inside.

After a while Theresa rubbed my back and offered me some water.

'I wanna speak to Grandma,' I sniffed as she held the glass towards me.

'No, honey. I'm sorry. You can't speak to your grandma right now.'

'I wanna speak to Mom then,' I said, biting my bottom lip.

Theresa swallowed and took me by the shoulders. 'You can't talk to your mom either, Nikki,' she said kindly. 'I'm sorry.'

And with that, I dissolved into a crying fit again. Why couldn't I speak to anyone? I felt so lonely. Where was everyone? What was going on?

After a while Dad came back in the bedroom and knelt next to me.

'I got your uncle Jerome on the phone, Nikki. You can speak to him if you like.'

I grabbed the phone as if my life depended on it.

'Jerome?' I said in a tiny voice.

'Oh, Nikki!' he said, his voice thick with emotion. 'I'm so sorry.'

I tried with superhuman effort to hold back the tears as I forced out the words.

'What happened, Jerome?' I pleaded. 'Where's Momo and Mellie?'

'Oh God, Nikki,' he said heavily. 'They've gone to heaven, honey. The Lord's taken them as His angels.'

'Why? Uncle Jerome – tell me! Why did God have to take them?'

'I don't know. That's His way and we none of us know the answer to that.'

'What happened?' I asked again.

'Oh, my little Nikki! I can't tell you. Please don't ask me to because I just can't.'

I started sobbing again. Jerome tried to comfort me as I bawled incoherently.

'Please Nikki – you gotta stop crying!' he said eventually.

'I can't!'

'You gotta. You just gotta be strong, honey. Please. For me.'

'I can't,' I wept, then my dad took the phone off me.

I don't remember how long I was curled up in a ball on my dad's bed before Theresa came in again. Time was moving in strange ways on this day. It seemed to stretch out then squash together. My world was coming to me in flashes and moments. Nothing hung together, nothing was real.

This time Theresa had Sere with her.

'Nikki...' Sere began, but then just rushed towards me to give me a hug. 'I'm so sorry.'

I accepted her hug and then pulled back – behind her stood David and Buddy, both looking awkward.

'We're sorry about your brother and sister, Nikki,' said David.

'Yeah, sorry,' repeated Buddy quietly. They both came and hugged me too.

I let them hold me briefly then I mumbled 'thanks' and curled up again on the bed. I couldn't look them in the eye or say anything more.

It wasn't them I wanted. I wanted Mellie and Momo.

After Theresa had ushered them out of the room, I sat on the bed just staring out the window.

By now the tears had stopped but the questions kept crowding in my head – what had happened? Did they suffer? I wish I knew. I wish I'd been there to stop it happening. Somehow, I felt like I could have prevented it if only I'd been there. I felt so helpless and isolated. I had to get out.

So I pushed myself off the bed, went to the bathroom and washed my face. I found Dad and Theresa in the kitchen with the other kids, tucking in to some macaroni cheese.

'Hey Nikki.' Theresa smiled encouragingly. 'You hungry? You want some food?'

I shook my head.

'I'm taking my bike out,' I said.

Dad looked up from his plate. 'Just be careful, Nikki, and don't be too long.'

But I was already heading for the garage where my bike was locked up. I needed to get out of that house – I needed some space.

I yanked open the garage door, picked up my black bike – a cast-off that used to belong to David Junior – and wheeled it out onto the street.

It was a warm, breezy evening and the street was already quiet after the rush hour had quietened down.

The street lamps hadn't yet come on and the sky was still lit by a fading orange sun.

I saw a mom struggling down the avenue laden down with bags of groceries, a few kids hanging around on the corner and a young couple holding hands on the bench opposite.

Everything appeared normal – the world looked the same as it did a few hours ago – but everything had changed for me.

I needed to feel the wind on my face so I got on my bike and pedalled as hard and as fast as I could up to the top of the block, pushing my legs down with fury with each turn of the wheel.

I gripped the handlebars and felt my lungs fill with air, breathing harder and harder as I turned round and rode all the way back down to the other end of the street, standing up in the saddle to get up more speed.

Then I turned my bike around and sat back down again. I let my feet rest gently on the pedals now as the bike rolled gently forwards. Every now and again I gave the pedals a brief turn, just to keep up the momentum as I let my panting die down and my heartbeat return to normal.

I looked up into the cloudless sky – the stars were just becoming visible against the darkening sky and I saw the milky outline of half a moon.

'Where are you Mellie? Momo?' I wondered out loud. 'Are you up there? Are you with God? Why? Why did you have to die? I don't understand. I don't understand any of it. Why am I here? Why can't I speak to Grandma or Mom? Did it hurt?'

I let the tears roll freely down my cheeks, not even attempting to wipe them away.

'I hope nobody hurt you,' I went on. 'I just want to cuddle you and let you know everything is going to be okay...' I must have talked to my dead siblings for at least an hour. Eventually, when it got dark, Sere came out and stopped me in the street.

'Dad says it's time to come in now,' she said. I let her lead me back inside and went straight to bed on the sofa in the living room. That was the first night in many where I cried myself to sleep.

The next morning Theresa and Dad hid the paper from me as I walked into the kitchen.

'What's in there?' I asked, my curiosity aroused by their obviously secretive behaviour.

'Nothing,' said Dad, irritated. 'Nothing for you to look at.'

What I didn't know then was that my mom's face was all over the local news. They didn't let any of us watch TV for a whole week after Mellie and Momo's death and nobody told me what happened or why they had died.

After about a week Dad got Grandma on the phone for me but she just cried a lot.

'Where's my mom?' I asked her. 'Why can't I see Mom?'

'Oh Nikki, you can't see her! You're not going to be able to see her a long while,' she said.

And that set me off again. I burst into tears.

After that day my life totally changed. I'd grown up with my brother, sister, Mom and Grandma and yet, in one dreadful moment, they had all been taken away from me. I don't remember much of what happened in the days following Momo and Mellie's deaths. I withdrew into myself, too shocked to speak to people, too grief-stricken to notice what was going on.

Before the deaths I spoke to Grandma on the phone every day but for that first terrible week of grief and pain, I was cut off completely. I was told that Sonny was okay, but I had no idea where he was. It was like everyone I'd loved had been taken away from me. And there were no explanations.

During the day I felt numb, indifferent to everything and everyone around me. At night, after lights out, I silently wept under the covers then fell into a heavy, spent slumber.

Frequently I dreamed of being with my brother and sister – going to the park together, playing on the swings or dancing round our old house in Brentwood.

Waking up, I'd feel a surge of happiness at having seen them both in my dreams – was this a sign? Did this mean they were both happy?

That good feeling didn't usually last long as the realisation sank in – I wouldn't be seeing them again. I would never again wake up with their small soft bodies lying each side of me.

This was it now. For the rest of my life I would always be alone.

Sometimes I just felt like going back to sleep so I could be with them again.

7

The Funeral

I CLUTCHED THE Pocahontas doll with one hand and gripped Theresa's hand with the other as we walked towards the funeral home in Brentwood.

There seemed to be hundreds of people in dark suits and dresses, milling around and talking in low voices. Some turned to look at me as we approached the front door to the funeral parlour but I didn't see anyone I recognised.

'Who are all these people?' I whispered to Theresa.

'Well, I can't be sure but I would guess many of them are your family, Nikki,' Theresa replied. 'I think they're from out of town – Georgia and Cincinnati. Don't worry – we'll soon find your grandma.'

Suddenly, among the throng, stood awkwardly by the door, I spotted Roland.

I couldn't help myself – I took off and ran towards him, shouting his name.

He turned just as I jumped into his arms and burst into tears.

He held me for a while then he gently put me back down.

'Come on Nikki,' he said quietly. 'Try to stop crying. Grandma's inside and she wants to see you real bad.'

It was the first time I'd seen any of my family since I'd been told of Mellie and Momo's deaths a week before but it felt like I'd been waiting months to see them.

Today was 1 July – the day of Mellie and Momo's joint funeral – and Theresa took me along as my father had to work that day.

'We better get your dress ready,' she'd said kindly that morning after the other kids left for school. 'Why don't you come with me and help pick out something nice to wear?'

We chose a royal blue dress with a frilly white collar and lace trim that I'd only ever worn for church. Later she carefully plaited my hair and polished my shoes so they shone. By the time she was finished I was smarter than I'd ever been in my whole life.

In the car on the way to the funeral home in Brentwood, I felt equal measures of nerves and excitement. Finally, I'd be able to see my grandma but I'd never been to a funeral before and had no idea what to expect.

The crowds were scary. How many people knew my brother and sister? If they all knew Mellie and Momo, how come I didn't know them?

It seemed so odd seeing all those strangers that when I found Roland I didn't want to let him go. He took me by the hand and led me through the entrance to a large hall where all the chairs were lined up facing the stage.

Already most of the chairs were filled with people. I recognised some of Mom's friends from Brentwood and my family from Brooklyn and Long Island. But there was no sign of Mom or Sonny.

There was a low murmuring in the hall, punctuated occasionally by sniffing and sobbing. A long line of people was waiting by the stage to go up to where two small white shiny boxes sat on a red velvet stand, surrounded by white flowers.

We walked slowly down the aisle until I saw Grandma. She was sitting at the very front next to the aisle. She was dressed in black with a large handkerchief in her hand. My grandpa was on one side of her, and looked like he was saying something to her but it was like she wasn't listening. She kept scanning the room, turning round to get a good look at everyone who was coming in.

My heart soared when I spotted her – as soon as she saw me she opened her arms and I ran into them. She wrapped me up tight and rested her cheek against my head, saying nothing. For the first time in ages, I felt safe and the tears just flowed out of me. She stroked my hair, kissed my head and wept helplessly, without any regard for the people all around. It was almost as if we were in our own little world.

We sat like that for ages while people came and went around us – many greeted Grandma by giving her a kiss on the cheek or telling her how sorry they were but Grandma seemed a million miles away.

Eventually Theresa came up beside her and knelt down next to us. 'Annie? You want me to take her up? To see them?' she asked my grandma.

I looked at Grandma and she nodded silently, pushing me off her lap as Theresa took my hand and led me to the line at the front.

Theresa had prepared me that morning for what would happen so I knew what was coming. She told me there would be open caskets in the funeral home and I'd be able to see my brother and sister one last time. She'd asked if there was anything I'd like to give them so I'd spent an hour carefully selecting the toys I wanted to give my brother and sister. I hoped now, as Theresa led me to see them, that I'd chosen right.

In the US, having an open casket is the norm and, whatever the circumstances, my family wanted to keep things as normal as possible. The caskets were raised up on a platform at the front and there was already a long queue of people ahead of us, slowly shuffling past.

Standing behind all these tall adults, my view was blocked out by large, suited bodies but occasionally I heard weeping and shocked exclamations escaping from the people in front. I tried peering round the side of the person in front but it was a big man and I couldn't get far enough round to see. Meanwhile Theresa had hold of my hand so I couldn't run up to the caskets.

It seemed to take forever but when we finally got to the front of the queue to see Mellie and Momo, I could feel Theresa's hand tighten around mine. She was tense, I could tell. But I wasn't nervous or scared – I was happy, excited even. I'd wanted to see them so badly. We stepped forward together and I climbed up onto the step to get a proper look – there they were!

Yet I almost didn't recognise them!

They were dressed in their best clothes – Mellie in a black suit and my sister in a pretty red dress – but their faces were covered in a strange brown, clay-like material.

I had no idea why they'd put the clay stuff on their faces – I could see it was supposed to look like it was their own skin, only they'd got the colour wrong. It was too dark so it appeared like my brother and sister had puffy tumours growing out of their faces.

I looked back up at Theresa for an explanation but she was racked with sobs and had her hand to her mouth.

I turned back, trying not to pay attention to the odd material, and pulled out the gifts I'd brought. For Momo I'd chosen the Pocahontas doll with the long dark hair and fringed brown suede dress. We loved to play with that doll so much – she came to all our best tea parties and we loved to brush her beautiful hair.

I could see that some people before me had already put some toys in the caskets at my siblings' feet so I carefully placed Pocahontas next to Barbie and Little Bo Peep. Then I took out the small white car I'd brought for Mellie and put that next to the toy gasoline tanker that lay at his feet.

As I pulled my hand out of the coffin, I let my fingers slide along the soft silky lining inside – it felt lovely in there.

And with their eyes gently closed, it seemed like Mellie and Momo were sleeping. Despite the strange things on their faces, they seemed really peaceful.

After a while Theresa gave a gentle tug at my hand to move me along, but I didn't want to go. I felt sure that if I stayed there long enough eventually Mellie and Momo would wake up and they'd shake off that dark stuff from their faces, jump out of the coffins and we'd all run out to go play together.

It hadn't been two weeks since the birthday party when they were cantering around laughing, shouting and so full of life. It made no sense that they should be lying here like this, unable to move.

Theresa tried tugging on my arm again but I didn't budge.

'Come on, honey,' she urged quietly. 'We gotta go back down because they need to start the ceremony.'

But I just stood there, a hand on each casket, unable to move, unwilling to leave my brother and sister.

'I don't want to go,' I said firmly. 'I shouldn't leave them on their own. Not again. Not ever.'

By now the tears had started up and I felt myself start to shake but I couldn't move if I tried.

Eventually Theresa took both of my hands and led me down the little steps. She had the full weight of my body against her as by now I was unable to stand on my own. Hands were reaching out to me but I was too far gone by this point and I felt only relief when my stepmom delivered me back to my grandma's lap.

Behind me I could hear various whispers: 'Oh, the poor child!'

'Debra's eldest girl – she wasn't there.'

'Does she know?'

'It's terrible – don't look!'

'Dreadful. Just dreadful.'

I buried my head in my grandma's bosom and let myself weep as the reverend from our Baptist church took the stand and started to talk.

'Today I feel all your grief and bewilderment as we gather to mourn the passing of Delvin King and her brother Melvin King,' he said. 'We will mourn their bodies – their souls rest with Jesus Christ.

'Children are supposed to outlive their parents and grandparents and there are many here who may question why innocent children suffer like this.'

A fresh wave of wailing started up but the reverend went on: 'God has his reasons. These children are God's Lilies of the Valley. And now they are Angels of the Heavenly Host.

'What has happened cannot change. All we can do is pray that He works it out.

'Today we must be careful not to rush to judgement. None of us here knows what happened. God will take care of the guilty.'

The reverend's words passed me by and eventually he stopped talking and the choir rose to their feet – it was a beautiful song and when I looked up I could see my mom's friend Carmen in the choir. But Carmen's face was a picture of misery and when they got to the chorus she stopped, put her hand to her mouth and turned away. She couldn't carry on singing through her tears.

The funeral went on but I don't remember much more of it – when it was over I looked up at my grandma.

'Where's Mom?' I asked her. 'When can I see Mom?'

'Your momma's gone, Munchikin,' she said. 'You're not going to be able to see her for a while.'

'I want my mom,' I repeated, pouting now.

'I know, I know,' she soothed.

After a while Theresa came to take me back to the car – I didn't want to leave Grandma but she let Theresa unhook my arms from around her neck.

'You be a good girl for your stepmom,' was all that she'd say. 'Your brother and sister are now in Heaven. They're with God so you don't need to worry about them no more.'

I was too exhausted to argue – at least I had seen my

brother and sister, no matter how much it hurt. I let Theresa lead me back to the car and I slept all the way home. When Theresa let me in the house that night I was like a zombie – I ate my dinner and went straight to bed.

'How is she?' I heard my dad through the walls.

'She'll be fine,' came the reply. 'It's been a really hard day but it's good she went. She got a chance to say goodbye.'

'Did you see Annie?'

'Yes, she looked terrible. I think they must have given her something. She could barely speak.'

'What about the caskets?'

'Oh David! They'd done their best but their little faces…!' Theresa's voice trailed off.

I must have dozed off early but later that night I woke to the sound of the TV blaring through the walls. My throat dry and scratchy, I crept out of bed to get a glass of water from the kitchen.

As I walked down the hall, I could see the flickering light of the TV bouncing off the walls in the living room.

I poked my head round the door, just to see who was watching, and was startled to see my brother and sister's faces staring back at me from the TV.

'A Suffolk police motorcycle detail escorted the funeral procession of Melvin King, five, and Delvin

King, six, to Pinelawn Memorial Park earlier today where the children were laid to rest.' A sombre voice intoned over footage of a hearse moving slowly down the street where I'd been only that day.

It was strange seeing my brother and sister on TV and I wondered to myself why I'd been taken home after the funeral instead of going on to the burial.

Then the picture switched to a grainy black and white shot of my mom and the voice-over went on...

'Mother Debra Roberson, 31, currently faces two second-degree murder charges for the deaths.'

I must have let out an audible gasp because at that moment Theresa and my dad, who were on the settee together, turned towards me and Dad shouted, 'Turn it off!'

But I'd seen enough – I knew what that meant. The TV said my mom had killed my brother and sister! No! No no no no no!

It couldn't be true – I didn't believe it.

I shot out of the room and dashed back to bed, my heart thumping like crazy, my head swimming. Theresa jumped up after me.

'Don't!' I heard Dad say. 'Let her be. Let her go back to sleep.'

But I didn't sleep much that night – I lay under the covers, shivering with shock and disbelief.

Questions swamped my mind – unanswered, un-answerable.

Why did they say my mom was facing charges for my brother and sister's deaths? It didn't make any sense – Mom wouldn't hurt us. She loved us. I always felt that she loved us – even when she was acting crazy and praying and shouting, I knew she wouldn't do anything bad to me, Mellie or Momo.

I had to know the truth.

The next day everyone acted normal around the breakfast table. Theresa hurried us all out of the house for school and Dad disappeared without saying anything special to me.

I knew there was no point asking them what had happened to Mellie and Momo – they had refused to tell me all along. And Dad thought I knew too much as it was. He always said that my mom and Grandma told me too much adult stuff, treating me like a grown-up instead of a little girl. I'm sure that this was his natural instincts – like most fathers, he wanted to protect his little girl from the horrors of the world.

I had to wait another week till I could speak to Grandma again on the phone.

After she asked me how I was doing at school and whether I was okay, I came right out with it: 'Grandma – did Mom do it? Did Mom do that to Mellie and Momo?'

There was a long pause and then the reply I'd been dreading: 'Yes. Yes, she did.'

No! It couldn't be true. I refused to believe it.

I lay awake that night, wondering what happened to Mellie and Momo and why they didn't look the same. And even though I was so young, it really hurt not to know.

I made up all sorts of different scenarios in my head about how my brother and sister had died – benevolent explanations, easy to imagine and easy to live with. Accidents that took place in a split second. Quick, painless deaths.

Mom never figured in any of these scenarios. I couldn't ever imagine that she was responsible for their deaths.

I guess my dad was right after all – I wasn't ready for the truth.

8

After

BEFORE MY BROTHER and sister died I was a really happy little girl – loud, outgoing, open and confident. It's true I had a smart mouth on me but at my dad's house I was learning when it was sensible to just keep quiet.

But after Mellie and Momo died, I changed. I couldn't feel connected to the people around me any more – Sere, David and Buddy had all grown up together, they all knew and loved each other. I was different – I'd entered their world as an outsider, a love child, a mistake, and I always felt like I carried the stigma of that with me.

The brother and sister I'd grown up with were now dead – and those who'd loved and cared for me all my life were gone. Nobody ever spoke about my mom, or Sonny for that matter, and I rarely got to see Grandma any more.

My whole life had been turned upside down. Everything I trusted as safe and strong had crumbled into nothing and left me alone in a world that was still very alien.

I became very shy and wouldn't speak to others. And above all I refused to share my feelings with those around me. If things upset me, I simply did not show it. I locked it away, turning my face into an impenetrable mask of blankness. Nobody could know what I felt on the inside because it was too dangerous to share it with anyone. Once upon a time I'd been open and loving but the people I'd trusted to stick around had gone, so now I didn't know who I could trust.

At nights, when nobody was there to see my pain, I'd cry myself to sleep.

And if someone's words stabbed through my mask, making it impossible to hold back the tears, then I'd calmly walk to the bathroom and allow myself to cry there.

Every time I cried to myself I felt stronger and more self-reliant – and those feelings were good. It was something deep inside that told me I needed to toughen up, to be strong or I simply wouldn't survive.

On the outside I was still a little girl – but within I felt like I was growing up at a million miles an hour.

The social workers started coming to the house not long after Mellie and Momo died. They were from Child Protective Services and I guess their job was to check up on me, make sure I was okay. Once a month there was a ring on the doorbell and then Theresa or Dad would poke their heads round the door where I was playing or doing my homework and fetch me to speak to them. I didn't like being the only one in the house who had to speak to them; it increased my sense of isolation, highlighted again that I was different to the others. But I did my best to try and answer their questions.

'Are you happy here?'

'It's okay – I'd rather live with my grandma.'

'Well, is anybody hitting you?'

'Nope.'

'What about school? How you getting on at school?'

'Fine.'

'Do you have any friends?'

'A couple.'

'Do you get on with your brothers and sister here?'

'Sure.'

On and on it went – the same questions every month. Sometimes I had a few questions of my own: 'I just want my mom to come home. I miss my momma. When is she coming home? Can you tell me when she's coming home?'

The reply was stark and uncompromising: 'Your mom's not ever coming home.'

That was one of those times I had to hold on really hard to stop myself from crying. I hated that social worker – she had no idea how hurtful it was to hear that my mom was never coming home. Didn't she understand how lonely I was?

But I bit back my tears and instead concentrated on the clock on the wall while she went on with her stupid questions.

Tick, tock, tick, tock... the little hand clicked round the dial face and I counted each second as it flicked by.

Hold on... I kept telling myself. *Just hold on.*

It was all so stupid and pointless – what good could they do now? Mellie and Momo were already dead – they hadn't saved them!

If they wanted to make me happy they could at least let me see my grandma – but no one seemed to care what I wanted. Apparently, because Dad didn't hit me, they had no reason to send me back to live with her.

Once I overheard my dad talking to them after we'd finished.

'She says she'd prefer to live with her grandma,' the social worker said in her gently patronising sing-song voice.

Dad snorted derisively. 'Of course she would say that!' he exploded. 'Annie spoils her rotten. Most children like people who give them everything they want.

'It's her grandmother! She doesn't know *how* to say "no" to the child. Just because there are rules and routines in this house, she finds that difficult. Well, I'm sorry but we're doing it for her own benefit and she might not like it and she might not see it at the moment but this is a damn sight better place for her than anywhere else right now. She gets treated exactly the same as her brothers and sister and she's damn lucky to have that. She's blessed!'

'Mmmmm. Yes, yes...' The long-skirted social worker seemed to be agreeing with every word my dad said.

It made me even madder and I slammed out of the house to ride my bike.

I guess to some extent he was right, but that wasn't the whole story.

It's true that in Dad's house nobody treated me any different, but I felt different. I called my stepmom 'Theresa' where all the other kids called her 'Mom'. She never offered to let me call her 'Mom' and I never asked. I guess it just didn't occur to either of us.

I had dead siblings and an absent mother – nobody ever talked to me about the people missing in my life and yet there was a great, gaping hole where once these people had been my emotional centre.

If I wanted to see my grandma, I had to beg my dad – and then, in the immediate aftermath of the deaths, he only let her come to the house. He wouldn't let me go to Coconut Street.

I don't know if he was scared of the memories it could bring back or whether he honestly feared for my safety, I just don't know. Maybe he felt that until the courts made a decision about my mom, he couldn't be sure one way or another. I never felt close to my dad in the same way I'd been close to my mom or Grandma. And the way he disapproved of me seeing Grandma made our relationship difficult.

If I wanted to see her or speak to her on the phone I had to ask him and if he said no, that was painful. I'm sure I wasn't the easiest child to talk to but at the same time, he wasn't a great communicator.

I missed the familiar people, the familiar places of my childhood – I felt abandoned and lost, like a little sailing boat bobbing around in a gigantic storm. There was nothing for me to hang on to any more and though I did like Theresa and appreciate her kindness, it wasn't the same as a real mom.

One time Grandma came over for a couple of hours on a Sunday afternoon, bringing with her a new Barbie doll and two dresses. We went to the park but the time seemed to rush away from us and soon it came time for her to leave.

After she'd gone, I was distraught, sitting on the front porch where I'd waved her goodbye with my head down on my crossed arms over my knees.

For once I didn't bother trying to hide my distress.

Twenty minutes later I was still sat in the same position and Dad came out to see me.

'Why are you crying?' he asked coldly.

'I want my mom. I want my grandma,' I bawled. I was just a little girl.

'Well, if you were living with your mom you'd be in the ground right now,' he replied flippantly.

That made me weep even more – no wonder I hid my pain from everyone!

I don't know if he meant to hurt me so badly that day but his words were like poison. She was my mom! She was everything I'd ever known and I knew in my heart she hadn't done anything wrong. No, she couldn't have done anything to hurt Mellie or Momo and anybody who said so was a liar!

It felt like everyone was trying to pretend that everything was normal but it felt strange the way nobody talked about Mellie and Momo.

Had they forgotten? Well, I hadn't!

I refused to forget about my dead brother and sister. I kept photographs of them in my school workbooks and was always grateful for an opportunity to talk about them.

Some friends at school already knew that they had died but others were curious when they saw the pictures.

'Who are they?' they asked.

'That's my brother Mellie and my sister Momo,' I'd say proudly, pointing to the pictures of their happy, smiling faces. 'She's a year younger than me and he's two years younger than me. We all grew up together.'

'Yeah? So where are they now?'

'They're dead.'

After a few weeks Dad told me to stop taking my pictures to school. I think one of the parents complained and it got back to the teachers. I just wanted to feel my brother and sister were with me all the time – when I had their pictures with me I'd talk to them in my head and it made me feel close to them again. It never occurred to me that I was freaking out my classmates.

Of course some kids, especially the older ones, already knew what had happened – after all, my mom's house was in Amityville and that's where we were still living and going to school. It was a small community and the death of two young children was big news. They certainly seemed to know more than I did and they weren't shy about approaching me.

'Why did your mom kill your brother and sister?' I got asked a few times.

I usually replied: 'Shut up! You don't know nothing!'

Mostly, they didn't mean any harm – they were just being kids. Those were the times I had to suck it up and wait till I got home to do my crying.

There was only one boy who actually teased me about it. One day in the playground at lunch he came up to me and started pointing and saying over and over: 'Your momma's a killer!'

That made me mad but I didn't have any trouble

shutting him up. I stood up from the bench where I was having lunch, swung my arm back and then let him have it! He fell down on my first punch and I gave him a couple of really strong kicks just to be sure he got my message.

'Shut up, asshole!' I spat. 'You wanna say anything else about my momma, you better come back with a lotta friends next time!'

I may have been quiet and I may have been shy but I wasn't afraid of using my fists. No, I was no pushover.

At that point I guess I knew somewhere way down deep inside me that my mom had something to do with Mellie and Momo's deaths, but I couldn't accept it was her who had actually killed them. I wasn't ready to let that possibility into my mind, so I imagined that everyone had got it wrong and one day there would be a simple explanation that would prove her innocence.

In the meantime, I took every opportunity when I was by myself to pray to God or talk to Mellie and Momo. Being alone gave me the space to think about my brother and sister, remember how they used to be: Momo's sultry pout, her angry little face and defiant manner; Mellie's sweet smile, his squeals of delight, easy-going personality and the charming way his tiny little hand would seek mine out when he was scared or lonely.

I'd think so hard about them I could almost conjure them next to me. Then I'd start speaking to them, telling them about my day, what was bugging me and how much I missed them both.

I never said any of this out loud – it was all in my head because I didn't want others to know I was talking to them. Sometimes I'd just be in the shower and whispering to them through the water.

I asked them questions too.

Under the covers, late at night, I'd ask Momo: 'Why did you have to leave? What happened? Show me what happened that day. Tell me who did it. Are you okay now?'

I was desperate to know what happened and I needed to feel they were safe now.

One day I plucked up the courage to ask my grandma on the phone: 'Did they suffer? Did Mellie and Momo suffer?'

'Yeah, they did,' she sighed. 'They really did.'

She could have lied, I suppose, but that wasn't like her. Hearing those words was excruciating but my grandma never hid the truth from me, however much it hurt. That's why I trusted her so much.

Another time we were on the phone and I begged to be allowed to see my mom.

'I just wanna see Mommy,' I cried. 'When am I going to be able to see her again?'

'You not going to see her for a long time,' Grandma said.

I started crying and she sighed with exasperation.

'Well if you gonna be crying when I tell you certain things then I'm not going to tell you any more,' she said. 'Your dad's already mad, saying I tell you too much. He's gonna stop me talking to you completely!'

That frightened me. I tried to stifle my sobs but the truth was hard for a child who was away from all the people she loved most in the world.

I wanted to know. I really did but it hurt so much. I tried my hardest not to cry and get upset when she told me certain things but I couldn't help it.

A few months after Mellie and Momo died Theresa took me to their graves in Pinelawn Memorial Park. I'd begged to go for ages and finally Theresa agreed to a visit.

I recognised the entrance to the park as I'd already seen it that one time on TV. The gardens were really peaceful; the flowerbeds were bursting with colour, the leaves shimmered all manner of golden hues on the trees, while the fountains sparkled in the early autumn sunshine.

We parked at the front then walked through all different types of gardens with sculptures, chapels, mausoleums and marble crypts until we came to a simple cemetery surrounded by rhododendron bushes.

There, Theresa led me to a single grave.

The gravestone was marked with simple writing:

Delvin King (1992–1998)

and

Melvin King (1993–1998)

The dates from their birth to their death were so close. It sent a chill down my spine.

It was lovely they'd been buried together. I knelt down and put my hand on the grass in front of the gravestone and started talking to them both in my head. It was so peaceful there I wanted to stay all afternoon but Theresa said we had to go home and after an hour she dragged me away.

'We'll come back,' she promised as she urged me to my feet. 'We'll bring flowers next time. Come on – your brother is waiting for us to pick him up from band practice. We're going to be late!'

I didn't care. I wanted to stay and be near my real brother and sister. But I didn't say that.

As it was I felt better when I went home that night. Something in me felt more peaceful knowing they were there in that beautiful place.

That night I talked to them both in bed.

'I'm going to come back and bring flowers next time,' I promised. 'Maybe when it's winter and there aren't any flowers in your garden. I'll bring some pretty, colourful flowers to cheer you up.

'And when I die I'm going to be buried next to you in Pinelawn. We'll all be together again.'

9

Dumb Dog

IN THE STILLNESS of the midsummer's day Nanny's rocking chair creaked loudly on the wooden slatted porch as she moved back and forth.

Creak, rock, creak, rock, creak, rock...

Nanny was my dad's mom and as she rocked I could feel myself being lulled into a kind of sleepy meditation by the relentless heat, the oppressive silence and the seesaw motion of the chair as it moved languidly across the floor.

Suddenly Nanny, who had been surveying us all through narrow eyes, exploded into life.

'David Junior!' she barked, pointing directly at my older brother who, like all of us kids, was leaning up against the porch railings, shielding his eyes from the sun.

'Yes Nanny!'

'Spell "essential"!' she ordered, repeating the word slowly so he could hear each syllable clearly.

'Right. Essential,' he started confidently. 'E-S-S-E-N...' There he paused and the creaking started up again. 'Erm...'

The pause seemed to go on a long time.

I glanced over at him. David's eyes were rolled upwards in his head, his brow furrowed in concentration as if searching out that part of his memory that housed the correct spelling for 'essential'.

He looked like he was struggling.

Aha! Suddenly this was interesting.

David Junior knew how to spell all of Nanny's words – he always aced her special Spelling Bees, which she regularly held over the holidays or weekends.

And he wasn't the only one who shone during those long, hot and difficult afternoons on the porch. My dad was one of five and his siblings all had children who were sent to Nanny and PopPop's with us during the vacation when our parents still had to work. I swear it felt like they'd all been raised on brain pills sometimes! They seemed to relish any opportunity to show off their vast vocabularies and frequently wound up competing on a level that was way beyond me.

Nobody had ever tested my vocabulary at home before. I suppose that for my mom and grandma, learning was considered necessary but not something you'd bring home with you.

So while all my cousins were happy to participate in the impromptu spelling competitions, they just filled me with dread.

I was eight, and used to being packed off to Nanny and PopPop's house in Wyandanch, New York to be put through our paces by Nanny, who was a strict but fair assessor. A retired nurse, she was a loving grandmother but upheld rigorous standards of discipline and education, believing wholeheartedly in the redemptive powers of progress. When it came to learning, she wanted to make sure that regardless of the grades we were bringing home, our minds were active and our spelling up to scratch.

I guess that's why Dad was so strict about our education.

Praise was meted out to those who got their words right but very little of it seemed to come my way. It wasn't that I was stupid as such – I'd just never been pushed in this way before so my skills lagged behind all the other kids, even Buddy who was a year younger than me.

Nanny wasn't cruel about it – she never laughed, teased me or punished me if I got the spelling wrong, which I frequently did. All she did was pause, while I waited to hear whether my guesswork had somehow miraculously led me to the correct spelling. Then usually she'd say: 'No, Nikkia. I'm afraid that's not right.' And she'd ask someone else to try it instead.

The embarrassment of being bettered by one of the other kids was usually enough to send the colour rising to my cheeks and my hands would clench in frustration and anger.

Worse, one of the others might let slip a snigger if my

spelling was particularly fanciful. Nanny would always tell them off about it at the time but later, out of earshot of the adults, I'd get teased mercilessly.

Oh, it would feel so good if Mr David Goody Goody Junior screwed up a word for once in his life. I sneered inwardly as I watched him struggle for the answer.

Come on. Come on!

I was willing him to get it wrong, just so that I could get my own back for once.

'T, I, A, L!' he finished triumphantly.

I turned to Nanny, expectantly – after all, I had no idea how to spell essential – only to find her nodding.

'Very good!' she smiled at him. 'The rest of you take note that if you think you're stuck, just pause, think about it, imagine the word in front of you and then try reading it. There's no rush – the important thing is to get it right.'

Nobody was paying her any attention – Sere was stood next to me, then there was Buddy, David, Kenny, Kason, Bruce, Charles and Rochae. We were all wilting in the oppressive city heat, hoping that soon we'd be allowed to break for a drink.

The creaking started up again – I let my eyelids fall closed as I felt my whole body relax against the porch fence. I could feel a great big yawn coming on and even though I tried to keep it down, it refused to go away. Finally I let my jaw slide open, my head roll back and I yawned heavily.

'Nikki!' Nanny snapped just as the yawn split my whole face in two.

I put my hand in front of my mouth and mumbled: 'Yes, ma'am!'

'I hope I'm not keeping you up! Perhaps you need a little nap!'

Nervous laughter rippled down the line.

'No, Nanny!' I objected. 'I'm fine. I'm fine.'

'Good – well, why don't you spell "cutie" for me then.'

'Okay – erm… Cutie. C-U-T-E. Cutie.'

Silence.

I looked at Nanny, expecting her to say I'd got it right, but she just stared straight back at me, her eyebrows raised quizzically. I glanced to my right, down the line of kids, to see some of them laughing silently into their hands. Finally David Junior erupted and the rest of them fell about like a bunch of hyenas.

'Stop it!' Nanny ordered, but it was too late. They were all cackling openly.

'Stop it, I said,' she repeated. 'Come on now – settle down. It's really not that funny.' Then she turned to me: 'Nikki, dear, don't you think you might have a letter missing?'

I made a face, as if to say 'Really?' then screwed up my eyes as if searching my brain for the missing letter but I couldn't think what it could be! I had no idea and the anger was steadily building inside me. What was the point of all of this? I felt like an idiot and Nanny wasn't helping at all – she was only encouraging the others to get a big laugh out of how stupid I looked.

Finally, exasperated, David Junior came to my rescue: 'Cutie has an "I" in it after the "T" and before the "E". Otherwise it's just "cute", not "cutie"!'

'Oh yeah, right,' I mumbled, feeling even more humiliated than before.

I just wanted to get out of there.

Nanny must have picked up on my discomfort as she took a quick glance at her watch and said: 'Okay, well maybe you're all a bit tired now. Why don't you go play for half an hour and then we'll have some lemonade.'

As she was saying this she eased herself up off her chair on the porch and waved us all to disappear into the yard where we could play.

I scuffed my foot against the porch fence and turned to face the road as David Junior came towards me.

'Jesus, Nikki!' he scoffed. 'You're such a Dumb Dog! She gave you a really easy one and still you messed it up! How did you manage that? You know, Nanny was trying to help you get one right. I mean, you haven't got one right the whole afternoon and then she throws you a complete slam-dunk and you screw it up! You Dumb Dog!'

'Yeah!' Buddy laughed. 'Dumb Dog!'

'Shut up!' I grumbled. 'Why don't you all just shut up. I'm not a dumb dog.'

Sere was by my side. 'Yeah, leave her alone. It's not her fault.'

I cursed myself for exploding like that – now he knew he could get to me. Until that point I'd been really careful not to rise to the bait whenever David tried to push my buttons. He still saw me as an intruder in their cosy family life and never wasted an opportunity to point out to the others and me how 'different' I was. Discovering my lack of spelling knowledge was like a gift from heaven and as soon as Buddy started repeating Dumb Dog, I lost it.

That night at home David Junior called me Dumb Dog over and over again, trying to get the others to mock me by inventing jokes about my stupidity.

'She's so dumb she doesn't even know how to spell "dumb"!' he cackled mercilessly. 'If you ask her to spell "I", she gets stuck! She tried spelling her own name yesterday – I think she can nearly do it today!'

The others tried not to join in but Buddy couldn't help himself; he cracked up and Sere smiled indulgently at her big brother's inventiveness.

It hurt me really bad. I felt like a caged dog at that point, I could have bitten his head off but, as usual, I kept it all in.

Later, in bed, I told Sere I hated being called Dumb Dog.

'So what?' she whispered to me across the bed in the

dark. 'So you can't spell very well? You can do lots of other things. You can dance really well and you're smart at other things. Just ignore him.'

But it wasn't just him. My dad's family was focused on becoming high achievers – after all, his sister was a lawyer, two brothers were in law enforcement and one was a car mechanic.

They set a lot of store by educational standards and fulfilling your academic potential. I honestly felt like I was the 'Dumb Dog' among them. It's a feeling I've fought all my life.

I attended Susan E. Wiley Elementary School, just like David, Buddy and Sere and, like my brothers and sister, my treatment at home was dependent on the report cards I brought back from school.

Unfortunately I wasn't a natural student. I struggled with English, I struggled with math and I struggled to get all my homework done.

'If you don't make your grades this term, I'm going to burn your butt, Nikki!' my dad threatened on more than one occasion. But he never carried through with it.

He wasn't allowed to hit me – the others got plenty of whoopings but he always spared me. I guess he was scared I'd tell on him to CPS and they'd take me away. Sometimes I wished he did hit me, just so I could get out from under his tyrannical rule and back to the soft, familiar warmth of Grandma's house. But other times, when I sat on my bed, listening to the screams of my brothers or sister as he whooped them, I was grateful my dad never raised his hand to me.

Of course I never knew for sure if he had enough self-control to abstain from violence – his temper was at times explosive and unpredictable – so the threat remained a credible and frightening one throughout my childhood.

'You done your homework yet?' he'd ask me sometimes when he came in from work.

'Sure,' I'd reply breezily, knowing perfectly well he'd probably seen my unopened school bag still strewn on the front porch.

'Don't you lie to me, missy,' he'd growl menacingly. 'I'm a cop. I know when you're lying.'

It annoyed the hell out of me. Of course I was lying! But I'd been able to get away with it before – why not now?

I'd roll my eyes at him dramatically but then I'd scurry out of the kitchen, grab my bag from the hallway and quickly take my homework to my room.

The fact was I didn't mind school – I certainly liked messing around with my friends – the work just seemed like an inconvenient drag that got in the way of socialising.

Later, at middle school, Dad got my teachers to report directly to him on my behaviour so I had a tough time playing up. But outside of the subjects I found difficult, there were lots of elements of school I enjoyed.

Theresa and Dad encouraged us all to develop our talents and Sere played the flute, which I thought was really cool. So they bought me a clarinet, much to their own annoyance, because to begin with, I did nothing but squeak. But there was something about the long black instrument with its springy keys and the wooden reed which I found entrancing and I persevered until eventually I could make a fairly decent sound with it. I loved learning how to play and read music, and over time I improved and eventually joined the school band.

In the meantime, I was forcefully 'improved' in every other way by Theresa and Dad, who refused to let me drift along the way I'd been doing before.

Theresa was the leader in our local girl scouts group so I was dragged along to that every week to take part in something I had no interest in like baking, sewing, outdoor activities or community service.

Sometimes I'd play up just for the sake of it. Like if she was taking a group I'd start talking really loudly to the girl next to me or walk out right in the middle of an important bit. If she asked me to do something I'd refuse or defiantly ask: 'Why?'

In my head, I'd smile inwardly. I was being cheeky and defiant, just like Momo!

Sometimes she reported back to my dad who put me on punishment. But it was Theresa who had to enforce

up screaming at her: 'When I get to be fifty
still going to be upstairs in this house
nothing!'

I feel bad about it now because I know I took advantage of her kind nature. I wasn't scared of talking back to her the way I was scared of my dad. So I took out all my rage and rebellion on her. Theresa never whooped any of us – she was a soft-hearted, peaceful woman and to be honest, she became the rock I clung to throughout the rest of my embattled childhood, during storms that threatened to truly engulf me.

After a while I self-consciously started to call her 'mi madre', 'my mom' in Spanish. I couldn't bring myself to call her Mom; I already had a mom. But I needed something closer and more intimate than simply Theresa.

As time went on I suppose it became obvious that I was starting to look like my mom, who was really pretty. We had the same slender nose, almond-shaped eyes and pouty lips. But at that young age, I didn't have any idea that I was good-looking. I felt different enough already without having something else marking me out.

I did my best to fit in at school, and tried not to let my insecurities about my cleverness show through. But we weren't helped by the fact that we were a poor family – not poor in the sense that we were on welfare but only just well-off enough to afford to buy our daily essentials and satisfy our educational needs.

Neither Theresa nor Dad worried too much about how we looked or what we wore – my grandma was good at getting me clothes – but generally we four kids didn't have anything nice that we could call our own. I turned up to school every day in well-worn hand-me-downs or the cheapest supermarket clothes, bought in bulk to save money on shopping for four children.

My one concession to fashion was given to me for my ninth birthday after much pleading and begging – a pair of knock-off Adidas trainers. They couldn't afford the real thing of course – they were $60, a fortune on our strict budget – but I was delighted to be taken to buy a replica pair from the market. They were my pride and joy and every morning I made sure they were cleaned and buffed so they looked as white as the day I first got them.

There was a small group of girls at school who didn't like me – maybe it was because I was starting to attract attention from the boys, I don't know. Certainly whenever I came home with a story of how they'd teased me or bullied me Theresa would always say: 'It's because they're jealous. Just ignore them.'

Well, I did try to ignore them but on this day they pushed me too far.

It was a couple of weeks after my birthday and I was wearing my new trainers. Nobody knew they were fake – you had to look very closely to see that they had four striped lines across the insignia instead of the usual three. But obviously these girls had taken a forensic approach to my appearance that morning in class and they knew.

Walking through the corridor on the way to lunch, the tallest girl, the leader, started to walk along beside me, her friends hanging back behind us, close enough to hear us.

'Nice Adidas,' she murmured sweetly. 'Are those real?'

I looked straight into her face and behind the innocent smile I saw the knowing smirk.

'Erm, I don't know,' I muttered back.

At that her friends erupted in laughter behind us and the leader gave a smug little grin. 'Oh, okay,' she shrugged, then she dropped back to her friends and they all started laughing uproariously.

She knew they weren't real – they all knew! They just wanted to show me up.

Bitch! I thought to myself as I felt the colour rising in my cheeks.

I was so goddamn pleased with those trainers, and she just made me feel like shit. My hands clutched my books to my chest so hard I could see the whites of my knuckles and I stormed off to my next class.

Later, after school, all the kids were hanging out in the gym area. That girl was there with her friends. *Now*, I thought to myself, *it's time to get your own back, now!*

So I walked up to her and just stood there, arms folded, right in her face, giving her the long, slow look up and down in that same catty, appraising way she'd done to me. It was such an obviously aggressive move the girls and boys around us fell silent as they looked at me. I waited until I had everyone's attention, then I asked, with one eyebrow raised and my hand on my hip: 'What's up?'

The other girls had fallen quiet too – they didn't expect this. I guess they were expecting me to shrink away and let them keep bullying me.

The girl seemed surprised but she was going to stand her ground – she couldn't let her fellow bullies see her look scared or getting faced-off. She took a step towards me so I could feel her breath on my face.

'Nothing, you ugly bitch!' she replied, eyeing me up and down, my challenge returned in her eyes. 'Why don't you mind your own fucking business!'

That was it – I launched myself at her, throwing my full weight behind a punch to the face. We fell on the ground and she started punching me back.

I felt a couple of blows to the head and side but I was clearly the stronger one and soon had her pinned to the floor as she struggled side to side to free herself. Before I could land another punch Buddy shouted for me: 'Nikki! Mom's here!'

I looked down at the squirming girl beneath me, her perfect hair now all mussed up, her spittle-covered mouth grimacing with fury, and I grinned.

'Just stay out of my face, okay?' I said. Then I rolled

off her and ran outside to join my siblings in Theresa's car.

Nobody said anything to me on the drive home – nobody would betray me in front of Theresa. They knew better than that – we all had our own battles to fight. I felt so alone in the world, if people faced up to me I had to stand ground on my own. There was nobody around to do it for me. I'd always been a tough little cookie, but what had happened in recent years was making me much stronger. The world could throw at me whatever it liked.

Time worked in that funny concertina way it does as a child – sometimes rolling by so slowly it almost seemed to stand still. Seconds, minutes and hours of brain-numbing boredom stretching endlessly away from me as if eons were crawling by. And yet the years themselves shot past in a flash. Before long it had been two years since I'd lost my brother and sister and seen my mom.

One Sunday, I was sat in my grandma's living room, watching TV and demolishing a ham sandwich, when she handed me a phone. She didn't say anything except: 'Here!'

I looked at her questioningly but then put the receiver to my ear.

'Hello?' I asked, thinking it must be my dad checking up to see when I was being dropped home.

There was a pause and then a woman's voice, hesitant, also uncertain: 'Hello?'

'Who's this?' I asked.

And then the words that made my heart leap.

'Is this my baby?'

It was my mother's voice! It was the first time I'd heard her speak in two years and here she was on the end of a phone, screaming with happiness and repeating over and over again: 'Oh my God! Nikki? I miss you so much. Nikki – my baby – say something! Is this my baby? I know this sounds like my baby! Say something to Momma!'

'Hi!' I said shyly, but I was grinning away. I had no idea where she was or why I was suddenly allowed to speak to her but it was wonderful just to hear her voice, and she sounded really good, so happy!

'Mom, I've missed you,' I said. 'Where are you at? Can I come and see you?'

'Not yet, honey, but soon. I'll see you real soon. Now tell me how you're doing? How's school? You being a good girl for your dad? Tell me everything!'

Tell her everything? It had been two years! I hardly knew where to start so I told her about taking up the clarinet and all my friends in school. I told her about living with Dad and Theresa and how I had too many chores. I didn't tell her about Dumb Dog – I don't know why. After a while I ran out of steam, then I asked, 'Are you coming back soon?'

'I don't know, honey,' was all she would say. 'Listen, I've got to go now but you be a really good girl and don't forget to say your prayers every day. Mom's going to stay in touch with you from now on. Grandma's gonna make sure of that – and you remember that no matter where you are or what you're doing, your momma loves you and always will.'

'Don't go, Mom!' I nearly shouted down the receiver as tears sprang to my eyes. 'I don't want you to go.'

It was too short. How many more years would I have to wait to speak to her again? I was terrified that if I put the phone down, that would be it; I'd never hear from her again.

'Don't worry none,' she soothed, though I could hear her voice thickening with emotion. 'Your momma loves you and we're going to see each other real soon. I promise. Okay?'

'Okay.' I smiled through the agony. I still trusted her, still loved her. She was my mom and one day we'd see each other again.

'Bye Mom.'

'Bye bye, baby.'

10
The Truth

I DON'T KNOW what made me look that day.

When I think about it, that day was no different from any other except that a nagging feeling had been building up in me ever since I'd first set eyes on the computers at my new school.

I was 10, just coming on for 11 when, like my brother and sister before me, I started at Copiague Middle School. Sere was there from day one to show me around, meet me for lunch and generally help me adjust to my new environment.

I quickly met a couple of girls who became firm friends and, as the weeks went on, I felt myself settling into the new routine.

At this school there were computers – computers with the internet. When I was first shown the IT room in the school, I was astonished – it all looked so high-tech, so advanced. I'd never seen anything like that before in my life. Four rows of eight smart, humming modern machines, all with access to the world at large. I'd seen computers before – my Nanny and

PopPop had one and we liked to fool around with games when we were at their house. But at middle school we were taught how to use them, how to research subjects on the internet and how to operate various applications that would help us with our studies.

And the central importance of computers to our schoolwork suddenly opened up a world of opportunity for me. We all had access to the internet from the computers any time we liked – if I had a question I didn't have to ask an adult, I could ask Google.

All the questions that had burned inside me for so long about what happened to my brother and sister could now be answered. As long as I sat down and searched I knew I could find out the truth that everyone had tried to hide from me. The real question is not why I went hunting for answers on that particular day but what took me so long?

I guess fear played its part. There had to be a reason nobody would tell me what happened and deep down I knew the truth wasn't going to be nice.

But I don't think anybody could have prepared me for what I found out that day... And just how much it did hurt.

When the time finally came it was a grey, cold and miserable day in early December, a few weeks after I turned 11.

I was sat at lunch, finishing up a chicken salad sandwich, thinking about my brother and sister. This wasn't unusual – I thought about them all the time. If anybody knew how much they occupied my thoughts, they'd have been shocked. I probably looked and acted pretty normal on the outside – but inside myself I lived in a ghost world, one occupied by two small children, long since dead.

I decided to try to find out more about how they died from the computers in the IT room.

Before now, there had always been a reason not to: I didn't have enough time, the computer room was full, I got caught up chatting to my friends. If I was going to do this, all the elements had to be right.

I checked the clock on the canteen wall – 12.15 p.m. I had nearly an hour before my next class at 1.05 p.m. Balling my sandwich wrapper into the trash, I took off for the computer room. It was empty.

At that moment I hesitated – I could easily have walked out right then and there, gone to practise my clarinet in the music room instead. But something urged me on that day. I could feel Mellie and Momo close to me.

Now, they were whispering. *We want to tell you NOW.*

My heart started beating like crazy. In just a few minutes I would know the truth.

I sat down at a console against the far wall – if anybody came in, at least I would have time to switch it off before they saw what I was doing.

I had every right to be there but still, I felt guilty. Up till then I'd been actively dissuaded from asking why my siblings had died so it felt like a major transgression to go looking for answers on my own.

I turned on the screen and the computer blinked into life – next I found the Google page. I put in the first thing that came into my head: 'The Murder of Delvin and Melvin'.

Nothing.

Next I put in my mom's name, Debra Roberson, and Amityville New York.

The first article on the page appeared to be a report from our local paper *Newsday* – I clicked through and started to read:

> A *Suffolk judge yesterday accepted a plea of not guilty by reason of mental defect from Debra Roberson, a 32-year-old Amityville mother who was charged with murdering her two young children, whom she immersed in scalding water.*

I stopped – I didn't know what immersed meant. I wrote it down and then opened another window and looked up the word immersed in the online dictionary. It read: Dip or submerge in liquid.

An involuntary gasp escaped from my lips as my heart froze in my chest. She drowned them? In scalding water? My mom did that?

My breathing quickened, my ears pounded as the blood rushed in. It felt like I was falling backwards down a long, dark hole... Falling, falling, falling...

There was nothing around me now – I was trapped in a vertical tunnel, unreachable to the outside world, locked in my private horror.

I read on:

When asked in court what she recalled of the evening her children died, Roberson said she remembered only that 'crazy things' had occurred.

'I just remember a lot of strange things going on, like things coming down the wall... and a man coming over and hugging him and kissing him,' she said.

Acting State Supreme Court Justice Michael Mullen, who accepted Roberson's plea in Riverhead, ordered her held for psychiatric examinations by Nov. 30, when he will decide whether to commit her to a mental institution. If she is found to be currently sane, she could be set free.

Prosecutors agreed with the plea, noting along with defence attorneys that Roberson had a history of mental problems. Two psychiatrists who examined her, one for the defence and one for the prosecution, both concluded that she was delusional when she allegedly killed the children.

The article went on to describe how in 1995 Mom was hospitalised for behaving irrationally and her children were taken by Child Protection Services, but when she was discharged, she got them back. Then, two years later on that fateful day in 1998, police broke into Mom's apartment and found Mellie and Momo on the sofa... Grandma had called the police after Mom had called her saying she thought Mellie and Momo might be dead.

The article then revealed the horrific truth:

Police said the children had burns on their arms, faces and bodies, and they found Roberson in a trance-like state, clutching a Bible, chanting incoherently and repeatedly crossing herself. Roberson's seven-month-old son, Hasson, was found unharmed, asleep on a bed in an adjacent room.

Autopsy results showed that Melvin died of asphyxiation and immersion in hot water, and Delvin died of asphyxiation, probably prior to being immersed.

I carried on reading about how at Mom's first arraignment, she was dressed only in a yellow tarpaulin that the officers had duct-taped her into because she'd taken all her clothes off in her cell. The paper had also found out that Mom had told someone at the hospital that she needed to 'boil the demons out of her kids'.

The tears fell silently as I read and digested every word of the report. So Mom had killed Momo and Mellie – that's what it said. She was insane and she'd done something terrible to them in the apartment that night.

Now I knew why my brother and sister's faces had been hidden under that strange putty – their faces, arms and bodies had been burned by the scalding water. God knows what they'd looked like under there!

No wonder nobody would let me see my mom – she was crazy. And a killer.

All this time, I'd never truly believed that my mom had harmed Mellie and Momo – I couldn't believe it. I knew that she loved us all. But here it was in black and white – she was insane, and a drug addict. The way they'd described her first appearance in court, I could just see it all – her shuffling, uncontrollable raving. I knew it was true.

The way they'd found her, trance-like, clutching a Bible, that day they found Mellie and Momo. It was true – it was all true.

They'd even locked her up before now and she'd talked about 'boiling the demons' out of the kids.

She'd wanted to kill us before!

I knew what happened when you scalded your finger just a little bit on hot water or a tap – you got a really big white blister and the skin underneath was red raw and bloody. I couldn't even begin to imagine how much

Mellie and Momo had suffered if she immersed them both in scalding water.

Now the sobs were escaping from me – I'd never ever cried at school, but I couldn't hold it in any longer. My hands instinctively wrapped themselves round my lower jaw, as if trying to stifle the pain, but nothing could silence the shock.

Oh, my babies! I wept inside. *My poor babies! How could she do that to you?*

My eyes just kept scanning those words on the screen: 'immersed in scalding water'. I couldn't tear myself away, yet I wasn't even seeing the words any more.

I was looking into the terrified eyes of my brother and sister as my mom raged and flew at them. I could feel their fear, the prickling dread on their skin and the awful feeling of helplessness as she picked up the huge pot of boiling water and threw it all around them.

In that moment, I felt the searing pain as it burned deep into their bodies.

They were dying – they were dying.

No, no, no, NO – I wanted to scream but I was frozen, locked to my seat, just watching the horrific events unfold in my mind's eye.

I'd seen them in pain before – when they got whoopings from my mom. I'd seen them frightened before, heard their terrified whimpering. It hurt me so much back then – but seeing this now was unbearable, heartbreaking.

I hated knowing the pain they had felt that day – hated my mom for doing it to them. How could somebody have it in them to do that to two beautiful kids? To their own beautiful kids?

I resolved then and there I could never speak to my mom again, not now, knowing what she'd done.

Suddenly a distant bell rang and I looked up; it was 1 p.m., nearly time for class.

The second sounding of the bell did its job, shaking me out of my trance. I jumped up, flicked off the computer and ran to the washroom to clean my face.

I hardly spoke to anyone for the rest of the day and after school I went home and I didn't tell anyone what I'd done.

I didn't need to hear any more lies, anybody trying to cover up the truth. I just needed time, time and silence to let the truth sink in.

Over the next week I went back into the computer room every chance I got.

I read the article over and over again, familiarising myself with the terms, with the people and what happened. I looked up the court system, how pleas work and what it meant to plead 'not guilty by reason of mental defect'.

I got the gist – it meant she did it but she couldn't be held responsible for doing it because she wasn't in her right mind.

So, she was guilty. That's all I needed to know.

Then I went looking for more articles. I found one written the day after the bodies were found from the *New York Times* that confirmed what I'd read and that neither teachers nor neighbours had seen Mellie and Momo for a week before the news broke.

It was like a jigsaw I was slowly piecing together in my mind. Brooklyn – that's the last time I'd seen Mellie, Momo and Mom. She had been out of her mind that day too but the next day was Monday – my brother and sister were meant to go to school but Mom hadn't taken them. The article was written on a Thursday, which meant that they had probably been killed on Wednesday.

She must have been off her head that whole time, I figured. Which meant that Mellie and Momo's agony and terror were not confined to one appalling moment in time. They had been stuck in that apartment for days on end, probably beaten, hungry, neglected, abused and terrified in equal measure.

Sonny was just a baby – how had he even survived those first few days, let alone the moment of madness that had robbed my brother and sister of their lives?

For the first time, I felt a surge of admiration for the tiny young boy who had lived through so much horror before he was even a year old.

Around six months after the incident, he had been returned to my grandma and was now a happy little four-year-old careering around, exhausting my grandparents with his energy and demands.

My one comforting thought was that I knew he'd have no memory of it. But why had he been spared when the other two were killed?

Why hadn't I been there to protect them?

More to the point – where were all the adults? My grandma? Grandpa? Social services? How had my mom been left to care for those three children on her own that week when even I, as a child, knew something wasn't right with her head?

None of it made any sense.

I found another article from *Newsday*, printed a few months after the court hearing where she submitted her plea. She was declared dangerously mentally ill and it was thought that the cocaine abuse had aggravated her condition.

I learned a great deal in that first year at middle school – but not necessarily in class. From the internet I learned all about drug abuse, cocaine, the court process, how social services work and what constitutes 'mental defect'.

Unlike my lost brother and sister, I did a lot of growing up that year. I allowed myself to accept what I read and I let the truth penetrate my very being until I was no longer able to deny the truth, to myself or anybody else.

Now, instead of waking up and seeing the faces of my brothers and sisters I'd open my eyes every morning and embrace the reality of what I knew as the truth: Mommy is a killer, I'd tell myself.

Mommy is a killer.

11

Running

'TIANA, WILL YOU take me to your house?' I asked my older cousin after the school bell signalled the end of the day.

I should have been lining up to catch the bus with my half-brothers and -sister at this moment but I'd made a momentous decision that morning to run away.

It wasn't a panicked, disorganised flight as you might normally expect from an 11-year-old. In fact, it was not so much running away *from* as running *to*. You see, I'd had enough of being lonely and isolated at Dad's house. I needed to be with my grandma.

I missed my grandma, I missed all my family – all the people I'd grown up with. Mellie and Momo were gone, Mom was gone too – perhaps I'd never see her again – the only people I had left to cling to were my grandma and grandpa. It was only with them that I felt safe.

Maybe everyone had expected me to just forget my past and move on but now, nearly five years after going to live with my dad, I was more miserable than ever before.

I wanted to grow up next to Sonny, playing and looking out for my little brother. I loved him more than anything in the world and I know he needed me.

So I'd made a plan – I went to school as usual that day and after class was over I tracked down Tiana, who was two years older than me.

'Sure,' she smiled. 'When do you want to go?'

'Today,' I replied, holding her gaze steady. 'Now.'

She laughed, fully expecting me to crack up too, like I'd made a joke.

Tiana was the daughter of my uncle Jerome's girl-friend Melissa, who had taken in my brother and sister when my mom was too unwell to care for them. I knew she had a soft spot for me and if anyone was going to help, it would be her.

'What? Why do you want to go there now? Don't you have to go home, Nikkia?'

'I'm not going home,' I replied, slowly and firmly. 'I have to go and see my grandma and your mom told me that if I ever needed help or anything at all, I should come to her. So, that's what I'm doing. And you've got to help me. Please. Take me to her.'

There was a pause as Tiana weighed up whether to take me seriously or not. She could easily have refused my request, but on the other hand, I had made it seem like if she didn't do as I asked, she'd get into trouble.

Without anybody there to verify my claims, she seemed to be at a loss. Perhaps it was something in the way I stared at her intently, or maybe she felt sorry for me because she knew what happened to Mellie and Momo. Whatever it was, she didn't take long to make up her mind.

'Okay,' she said reluctantly. 'But I can't take you on the bus.'

I was so relieved the first part of my plan had worked that the words came tumbling out of me. 'I know. I know. They'll just throw me off. I've thought of that. We can get a taxi – I've got some money.'

In fact, all I had was my $1.50 lunch money – but Aunt Melissa only lived in Amityville so I felt certain we had enough to take us from school to her house.

Tiana flagged down a cab and we both got in – the light flicked on and the red meter instantly lit up 75 cents. My heart started thudding – we hadn't even started and already that was half my money gone!

Tiana caught my panicked look. 'Don't worry – I've got some money,' she smiled.

The total fare came to seven dollars – luckily, Tiana had another five dollars and the taxi driver let us off the fifty cents we were short.

Part one successfully completed, now I had to put into action the next part of my plan – convincing Aunt Melissa to take me to Grandma's house.

As we climbed the staircase to the fourth floor of their block in Amityville, I caught the smell of fried chicken wafting down from the apartment. It already smelled good to be free!

'Mom!' Tiana yelled after letting us both in with her key. 'Mom! Cousin Nikkia's here!'

Aunt Melissa suddenly appeared at the entrance to the kitchen. 'Nikki?'

Just seeing her face and hearing her call my name was enough to reawaken all those hidden feelings of loneliness and abandonment that I'd been suppressing for so long. The familiarity of the apartment, her voice, the smells. It was all too much – this was a place that had been part of my world five years ago. I'd been a regular visitor here during those turbulent years when Mom failed to give us a stable home life. But since I'd been at my dad's house, I hadn't visited here once.

I ran into my aunt's embrace and sobbed heavily.

'Honey, what's wrong?' She pulled me away to look into my face, as if searching my features for the answer. 'Has something happened? What's wrong? Tell me!'

Aunt Melissa had enough on her plate with five of her own children – I didn't want to stay here, or be a burden to her, so all I said was, 'Nothing's happened. I just want to see Grandma, that's all.'

'But why?'

'I just wanna see Grandma...' I repeated. 'Nothing's happened. It's just... I just don't want to go back to my dad's house.'

Then I started weeping once more and Aunt Melissa said: 'Okay, okay... listen, don't worry. Here, have a soda. Sit down with Tiana and the others and I'll get your uncle Jerome.'

I went through to the kitchen with her – two of her youngest were playing on the floor so I bent down to play with them. I loved seeing my younger cousins. Just being around babies and young children made me happy.

Within a few minutes we were engrossed in building a tower of bricks and I overheard Aunt Melissa on the phone to my uncle.

'Jerome? You better get down here. Nikki's here... I don't know, she won't say. She just turned up after school with Tiana. Says she wants to see Annie... No, she seems fine. Okay, okay. See you soon. Bye.'

And there it was – part two completed. I'd lied to Tiana when I told her that Aunt Melissa had agreed to help me – I don't think she ever said anything of the kind, but she had said that she'd always be there for me. So I took her at her word. And I knew that if I got to her in Amityville, she'd help me get back to my grandma's. With Uncle Jerome on his way, I felt closer than ever to getting back to Grandma. Back to my real home.

I guess he came as fast as he could from Brooklyn but it was still an hour before he arrived.

As soon as he walked in and saw me, he came over to where I was sat in front of the TV and gave me a big squeeze: 'Come on, Pumpkin,' he urged, motioning me to go have a private word with him in one of the bedrooms. 'Let's have a talk.'

I followed him into Aunt Melissa's bedroom where he sat on the end of the bed and I sat in a chair opposite.

'Nikki,' he said seriously. 'What's wrong? Why did you come here to your aunt's house?'

'I want to live with Grandma,' I said.

'But why? Don't you like it at your dad's place?'

The tears started to fall but I swept them off my cheeks defiantly. 'He's mean,' I explained. 'I hate it there.'

'Does he hit you?'

'Uh uh.' I shook my head. 'But he might. He gives the others whoopings and they're real bad. He makes them undress so it hurts more. I'm scared of him.'

'You know your grandma isn't allowed to take you,' he said slowly. 'If she could have she would have taken you all them years ago, when Mellie and Momo died. Your dad has custody of you and she could get into trouble if you just turned up at her place without making arrangements with David.'

'He doesn't let me see her none anyway!' I cried out, my voice raised from the outrage and injustice I'd been harbouring all these years.

I'd reached breaking point and the emotion forced a passionate fluency out of me. 'She' s my grandma but he only lets me go over there sometimes, and only when he feels like it. And I have to ask him like it's a big favour he's doing me but he doesn't always let me so I'm scared to ask in case he says no. What right has he got to stop me seeing my own grandma? I didn't even know who he was until he came to get me when I was seven! He doesn't talk to me, he just comes home and shouts at us all. I don't even think he likes me. I hate him and I don't want to see him again!'

Jerome held my gaze, silenced by my uncharacteristic outburst. He had known me all my life and while I could be a smart-mouth and answer back, I don't think he'd ever seen me like this before, inflamed with anger and passion. Maybe he'd never realised how hard it was for me – maybe he wanted to help.

He took me in his arms and rocked me gently as he tried to hush the loud sobbing that now escaped from deep inside.

'Shhhhh…' he soothed as he stroked my hair. 'Shush now, Nikki. Look, I'll call your grandma, okay? I don't know what she can do today but you're right. You've lost too much already, baby. You should be able to see her whenever you want.'

So my grandma was called and again I ranted and railed at her, telling her over and over how unfair it all was.

She nodded and tutted and sighed and cried with me – but at the end of it all, she told me I had to go home to my dad.

'I can't do nothing about it, honey,' she said sadly,

shaking her head. 'Your dad ain't done nothing wrong. If he'd been hitting you then I'd call CPS like a shot. Believe me, I wouldn't stop for a minute. But he knows that as long as he doesn't hit you then we got no reason to stop you living there. I know it's hard, baby, I know. Grandma misses you too. But you just got to be asking your dad if you can see me and don't be scared none if he says no. He ain't gonna hurt you.'

Nobody seemed to understand – I didn't have to be beaten or punched to feel pain. The rejection was enough to wound me deeply. Worse, now I was being sent back to him, I'd be in big trouble for running away in the first place. I cried hysterically and clutched at my grandma as if my life depended on it.

'You really think I want to do this to you?' she said, wiping away her own tears. 'Please, Nikki honey – don't make this impossible for me. I got so much pain in my heart right now, I can't bear the sound of you crying no more.'

Eventually, worn out and worn down, I allowed Uncle Jerome to drive me back to my dad's house later that night.

Dad didn't say a word to me when I came in but I felt the anger from his cold gaze like a hard slap.

Theresa gave me some hotpot they'd had earlier and then I went to bed, defeated and depressed.

That night I cried myself to sleep again – but these

were tears of frustration. In my heart I felt so old, yet in years, I was still just a child with no more power to influence my life and surroundings than a leaf blown in the wind.

I felt helpless and small.

The next morning Dad left for work without saying a word to me and it was Theresa who explained the situation.

'We're putting you on punishment,' she said. 'No more TV, no more playing outside and an extra hour's chores every day for a week.'

I didn't respond – what was there to say? I'd been expecting this.

What I hadn't expected was Dad's complete silence. He didn't talk to me for a long time after I ran away.

One day about a fortnight after my attempt to escape, I was sat at the kitchen table, making a stab at my math homework when I asked Theresa if Daddy was still mad at me.

'He's not mad any more,' she sighed. 'He's upset. He was really hurt when you ran away. We both were, but it was worse for him. He's doing his best, Nikki. He wants to give you the same chances in life as your brothers and sister. I know he doesn't show it very often but he does love you. Very much. You running away... well, it hurt his feelings.'

I didn't understand – didn't he ever consider my feelings?

Every day I woke up without Mellie and Momo, without my mom. Every single day I woke up to a world that was already painful and difficult. Why did he make it worse for me?

But I didn't say any of this – I wasn't after sympathy.

'I just want to see Grandma,' I offered limply. 'Why does he make it so difficult?'

'It's for your best interest,' she repeated.

Maybe it was – maybe he was right all along. All I knew was that in keeping me from the only person I knew and loved all my life, he made me hate him.

I couldn't figure out my dad – on the one hand he didn't seem to show me any affection, on the other he was determined for me to stay with him and not let me be with my grandma, who truly loved me. Theresa said he loved me but I never heard it from his own lips.

His actions seemed as baffling to me as his strange, changing eyes. They could flip from grey to green to blue, depending on the weather. If it were sunny outside they'd be bluey-green and if it were dull outside they'd be grey. You could tell the weather in my dad's eyes and I think that's how I felt about him in general.

Sometimes he was all nice and easy to get along with but at other times he'd be angry and there seemed to be no good reason for it. I'd look into his eyes to try and gauge what kind of mood he was in – and depending on his mood, what kind of day the rest of us could expect.

My dad's eyes were my own personal weathervane.

My stepmom loved me – I didn't doubt that – and to this day I feel I can talk to her about anything. But at the time I wasn't really close to anyone except Sere and the two boys. All of us lived in fear of Dad.

He must have thought he was doing the right thing but I couldn't see it. I just couldn't see it. I grew up angry, upset and miserable.

12

Mom

ONE GUSTY MARCH afternoon, when the leaves were blowing all around, Grandma told me the news. We'd just had Saturday lunch on one of the rare weekends I was allowed to stay at her place and I was at the table, finishing off a large bowl of chocolate ice cream.

'You wanna see your mama?' she asked, a big smile playing on her lips.

My heart leapt. 'Yes!' I screamed.

'Well, we can take you to see her tomorrow,' she went on. 'There's a family day at the centre and we've been through court to allow you to come along.'

My head started swimming with the prospect of what lay ahead the next day. It had been so long – four years – and despite everything I'd read, despite knowing the truth, I still needed to see her.

She was my mom – at 11 years old I missed her more than ever and I couldn't imagine never seeing her again. But almost immediately after the excitement, the fear flooded in.

'Will it just be us going?' I asked tentatively. I knew

now my mom was a killer – what if I froze on the day? What if I couldn't speak to her? A large part of me despised her still and I didn't know if I even wanted to talk to her after learning what she'd done to Mellie and Momo. If it was just the two of us, I didn't want to go.

'No, honey,' my grandma laughed. 'There's lots of us going – I'm taking Sonny too.'

That night I lay awake in the darkness, tracing the shadows on the wall with my fingers and letting my mind wander over the day ahead.

I knew where we were going – Mid-Hudson Forensic Psychiatric Center. I'd read about it in the papers and I knew that it was a high-security hospital for people who were really sick in the head.

I just couldn't imagine it in my mind. Neither could I picture my mom there. I'd seen a photo of her in the paper, taken just after she was arrested that night in 1998, and she was like a zombie, eyes staring blankly ahead, face set, expressionless. I'd seen it for myself many times when she appeared lost in a world of her own.

How will she be tomorrow? I wondered. *Will I be faced with a zombie?*

I had no idea. The way they'd described her in the newspaper reports seemed so strange.

And what would she think of me? The last time she'd seen me I'd been at least a foot shorter. I'd changed a lot in the past four years, and not just on the outside.

She killed Mellie and Momo, I whispered to myself in the dark.

She didn't mean to do it, she was out of her mind – I was replaying the conversation to myself that I'd had so many times before in my mind.

Ever since I'd read the reports on the internet about what she'd done I'd fought a terrible internal struggle for my mom's soul. I couldn't forgive and forget but neither could I abandon her entirely.

I had to find out the truth from her for myself. I had to hear it from her own lips.

I told Grandma about what I'd read, but whenever I spoke to her about it, it seemed like she couldn't face up to the truth.

'Grandma – the newspaper said she was out of her mind on drugs,' I said.

'Yes, that's what it says,' she'd nod. 'But I don't know how she could do that. She wouldn't do that to your brother and sister. She loved them.'

'But maybe she wasn't seeing them there,' I pushed on. 'Maybe in the moment when she killed them, she just saw the devil standing there.'

'Mmmm hmmm,' Grandma nodded again. 'That's what them doctors and lawyers says. They say she didn't know what she was doing.'

'What do you think, Grandma?'

'Me? I think the devil took your momma's mind. I don't know. I don't know what to think. I just gotta keep helping her because I know she a sick lady.'

And that was it – the only person who knew for certain what happened that dreadful night was Mom and, one way or another, I resolved I was going to find out the truth from her.

Still, I was nervous as hell. What would I say to her? What would she say to me? Would she want to hug me? Could I do that? It all played over and over in my mind that night as I prepared to meet a real-life killer. My mom.

The next morning I showered early and dressed in the clothes I'd laid out the night before. My favourite red sweater, jeans and sneakers. They weren't particularly good clothes but they were the ones I liked the best on me and I felt better wearing nice clothes for my mom.

It took about two hours to drive from Grandma's house on Coconut Street in Long Island to the Mid-Hudson Forensic Psychiatric Center in New Hampton, upstate New York.

I could hardly contain myself, my emotions were running wild that morning. I was nervous, scared and happy all at the same time.

I helped get Sonny ready in a sweet blue outfit while we waited for everyone else to turn up. Seeing as it was family day, Mom could have as many visitors as wanted to come so we were going in a big group with a couple of my grandma's sisters, my uncle Jerome and a few of my cousins.

The journey seemed to go on for miles and miles as we left the built-up urban sprawl and headed out into the open expanses of the interstate 87, past the New Jersey Turnpike onto Route 6, through the small towns of Chester and Goshen then up into the outskirts of Middletown in New Hampton.

I let the changing scenery wash over me as I prepared myself for what lay ahead. I didn't feel like talking to anybody so I just kept my head pressed up against the window and my eyes focused outside the car.

After a couple of hours, we pulled off the interstate and up a long driveway – suddenly a smart collection of red-brick buildings came up into view. Even from a distance away, I could see they were massive. My heart-beat quickened – in front of me was an enormous, sprawling complex of anonymous-looking buildings with a barbed-wire fence all around. To me, it looked like the prisons I saw on TV – large, intimidating, impenetrable.

We parked up and then began to walk towards the entrance – now I could see people walking around behind the fence. My heart did another somersault.

Oh my God, what if she could see me right now? There were hundreds of dark windows in each building – was she looking through one of them? Did she know we were here?

Grandma had told me the night before that Mom had been prevented by the courts from seeing me all this time and that she had had to fight to allow me to come visit her.

'She really wants to see you honey-pie,' Grandma reassured me. 'Your momma would move heaven and earth just for a chance to give you a hug.'

It felt nice to be told that – but at the same time I couldn't help being scared.

I held tightly to my grandma's hand as we entered the main entrance of the largest building on the front and our bags were searched as we went in. Grandma had brought my mom a large pizza and they even looked inside the box!

Then we had to go through security ourselves; first of all we went through a metal detector one at a time and they made me take off all my jewellery with pointy tips like my earrings, and I had to go through several times before they were happy.

'Why do we have to take off our jewellery with pointy tips?' I whispered to Grandma. But she didn't answer, just hushed me, as she took direction from the large security officer busting out of his uniform.

We were shown to a locker where we could store all our jewellery before we were finally allowed through to the main room.

Suddenly I grabbed my grandma again – was this it? I didn't know if Mom and the other patients would be waiting for us in the hallway when we arrived so I steeled myself to come face to face with my mom.

*

But as we entered the large cafeteria-like room with high ceilings I could clearly see that there weren't any patients here yet, just lots of excitable families with tonnes of fast food brought in as a 'special treat' for their loved ones.

Although there were lots of people around it wasn't too noisy – it felt like everyone was holding their breath, waiting, keeping a lid on things.

Grandma got us all settled at a long table and I distracted myself by looking after Sonny – by now it was around 11 a.m. and I was bursting to use the toilet. I saw a sign to the bathroom pointing down a long corridor, so after 15 minutes I decided to take myself off there.

I was halfway down the long corridor when ahead of me I saw a large collection of men and women turn the corner. They were dressed in normal clothes but even from a distance, I could tell they were 'the patients'. It was something in the way that they moved all together, not like a collection of adults, but like a line of school-children being taken on an outing.

The way they marched towards me, in a crocodile line, they could have been holding hands. The line just went on and on and on – there must have been about 100 of them!

I stood there, frozen to the spot, unable to move

forward towards the line of patients walking towards me and also unable to run backwards.

Somewhere in that line was my mom. Had she seen me already?

Eventually, fear got the better of me and I turned and ran back to our table. I didn't want to see her. Not like this – not on my own!

The large room full of families fell into complete silence as the patients entered and lined up against the far wall. Then a man with a clipboard who was clearly in charge went down the line, ticking off the names of the patients and ushering them forwards, towards their families.

Small, isolated pockets of laughter and chatter started to spring up around the patients reunited with their loved ones.

My stomach was in knots as I scanned the line intently until finally my eyes landed on my mom!

She was wearing a white sweater and blue jeans, and her eyes were smiling with such warmth and love, I couldn't help myself, I started smiling too.

As her name was called out she practically ran towards us smiling and laughing – just as I remembered her from the good old days.

Grandma was also up on her feet, walking towards Mom, and the pair met in the middle of the room in a fierce embrace.

Then Mom came bounding over to me – I was so scared I was shaking.

'Oh my baby!' she cried, her voice rising to an over-excited shriek. 'Come give your momma a big hug!'

But I couldn't. I couldn't move. I didn't want to give her a hug. I didn't want her to touch me with her hands.

She put her arms around me anyway and squeezed me tightly.

My arms were still pinned to my side – I couldn't move. She let me go quickly and then held me in front of her, drinking in the sight of me with a great big grin on her face.

'Oh, look at my baby!' she breathed. 'You so grown up! You look like a young lady already.'

As soon as she let me go, I slid across the bench to the other side of the table and sat down at the opposite end from where she was sat. She must have sensed my reservation because she didn't follow me and she didn't make any comment. She just let me sit next to my grandma.

I let the conversation around me take off as all my uncles and aunts offered their good wishes and proffered the food they'd brought.

Jerome told my mom how well she was looking – and I guess she did look well. At least her face was expressive, her eyes bright and she was full of smiles.

She seemed a little puffier around the cheeks and maybe she'd put on a few pounds around the hips but she was still beautiful and the excitement was just bubbling out of her.

But I couldn't stop staring at her hands – those hands that traced and drew the conversation through the air, that fluttered around my mom's head, face and neck, that refused to sit still on the table as they clutched other people's hands and squeezed shoulders affectionately. These were the same hands which killed my brother and sister. My eyes were glued to them.

After about ten minutes Mom looked straight at me and smiled.

'Come here, Nikki,' she said in a soft voice, patting the bench next to her. 'Why don't you come sit by me.'

I couldn't resist. It was something in the tone of her voice, so soft, so mellow. Mom wanted me close to her and for so long I'd yearned to hear her tell me that she loved me, that she missed me. Longed to feel her arms around me.

I got up and sat beside her and she put her arm around me and for the first time in years, I felt good.

We sat like that for a while as Mom chatted with everyone at the table, making us all laugh with her stories about what she got up to in the hospital.

She was on sparkling form, entrancing, captivating, charismatic, and it felt good just being close to her as she held the whole table's attention with her ridiculous impressions of the other women in her room or the hospital staff and the way they bossed her around.

After a while I finally went to the bathroom and when I came back, Mom was tucking into some pizza and my uncle was handing round sodas.

She turned to me then and asked me how I was doing.

'How's your dad?' she enquired, munching through a large bite of pepperoni pizza.

'Fine,' I said, still a little shy.

'And what about your stepmom? You get on well with Theresa?'

'Yeah, sure. She's really nice,' I said.

I didn't want to tell her too much – after all, it felt like we were still strangers to some extent.

After a while she finished off her pizza and grabbed a deck of Uno cards and we had a couple of games. Then we played a few rounds of Yahtzee before getting stuck in to a seriously long game of Monopoly.

I didn't said much on that first visit – I certainly didn't bring up Mellie or Momo. It didn't feel right – I knew one day I'd get to the truth but for now it just felt enough to be sitting in my mom's company.

She seemed so normal, so clear-thinking and together.

We were there for hours, just talking, eating and playing games, but around 4 p.m. the staff started ushering the families out and we had to pack all our stuff up.

Mom seemed really upset but I could tell she was trying to hide it.

'You gonna come and see me again real soon?' she asked me. I nodded eagerly.

'And I'll write to you,' she promised. 'Maybe you could write to me too. It's so good to see you, baby. I've missed you so much.'

At the end, Mom made us all join hands and say a prayer together.

'Oh Lord,' she raised her voice upwards with her eyes closed. 'Bless this beautiful family and keep them all safe and close. Keep love in their hearts and close to you, Father, so they may know the joy and happiness of your love. Bring them safely back here soon, oh Lord, so that we can all be reunited. And may I one day be allowed to come home and be a good person in society. Amen.'

'Amen,' we chorused quietly.

Mom turned to me. 'You say your prayers every night, Nikki?'

'Sometimes,' I replied.

'You should pray every day, honey,' she said seriously. 'Pray for God to show you the right path and pray for your momma. Pray they let her out of here soon so we can all be together again.'

'I will, Mom,' I said, my voice quiet and shaking with emotion. I didn't want to leave her in this place. This time I threw myself around her in a gigantic hug, pressing my body against hers and squeezing her tight.

She squeezed me back, then pulled away and stroked my face with a smile.

'Be a good girl for your daddy and Theresa,' she said smiling. Then she picked up Sonny and gave him a squeeze, covering his messy face with little butterfly kisses.

When we left I turned back to see her smiling and waving, calling out to me: 'I'll write to you baby!' but I could tell she was really upset. I hated it, hated leaving her.

After we'd retrieved our jewellery from the lockers, I held Grandma's hand as we walked towards the car. Nobody said a word – everyone was upset.

All the way home, I felt awful, not knowing when I'd see my mom again. But at the same time something in me was happy too – she was still the same Mom I remembered. Maybe she was a little thicker round the waist but it didn't matter. She was my mom and the love I remembered was still there too.

Grandma dropped me at my dad's house and I ran straight to the bathroom, where I sat on the toilet and cried. The tears were forced out by a conflict of emotions. My mom was still a killer and I hated what she had done, but at the same time, I could still feel love for her deep down inside. I just didn't know what was the right thing to feel. Could I ever forgive her?

Every minute we'd driven away from Mid-Hudson Forensic Psychiatric Center had taken me further away from my mom. Now here I was, lost and alone, without her once more.

13

Letters from My Mom

I MAY HAVE been back in the real world without my mom, but she never forgot about me, not for one minute. And now that the courts had granted her access to me, she kept her promise and started writing letters and calling the house. She wrote me constantly and I kept every single letter. Here are a few of them.

2 May 2002

Dear Nikki,

May peace and blessings be upon you and the family. I pray by the time you receive this letter you are in great spirits. As for me I'm in a wonderful mood. I just came from one of my groups over in the mews building. We are always in some groups or something. But I like it that way. It's better than sitting around doing nothing.

I have been trying to call you. I can't stand when I miss speaking to you.

I wish you had your own cell phone – but like I said we are in each other's heart.

Although I'm not there physically I'm there

emotionally. Precious Angel, we are going to have a good life.

All those things I had when I was out in the world. They were not meant for me to have. Reason being they were not centred in Christ. Now I have a solid foundation.

My life is in God's hands. When He sets me free life is going to be so very beautiful.

There is a story in the Bible. It is Job. It's about a man that lost his entire family and all his riches. Although he lost everything including his health he never lost faith in the Lord. In the end God gave him even more than he lost. You want to know why? Because he never lost faith.

Baby girl, right now your mother is walking by faith not by sight...

Trust me, sweetheart, it's going to get better. Your mom won't be locked up forever. Just know that God loves you and of course Mommy loves you. Keep on praying and don't stop. God may not answer our prayers when we want him to but he is always on time.

Love, Mommy ☺

16 June 2002

Dear Nikki,

May peace and blessings be upon you and the family. I pray by the time you receive this letter you are in great spirits. As for me I'm doing well I must say today. I made it through those two birthdays.

Thank God it is over until next year.

So how are you, sweetheart? Nikki do you understand how much you mean to me?

I'm looking forward to the day we are eating dinner together at my favourite restaurant.

My first day home for good I will be going to the cemetery to place roses in that vase you were telling me about.

Roses are my favourite flowers. Then I want us all to go to eat. Then come home and just praise God for allowing the day to be possible.

Baby, let me tell you what has been going on in this dump. There is this woman that works here that acts as if she is in love with me.

I had to report her two times already. The first in 1999 when I came here for my evaluation. The second time for touching me. She still hasn't learned her lesson. That is because they didn't do anything about it. She is very fat with these big breasts and she has the nerve to put those on my back.

She works on my last holy nerve. I get upset at times because she thinks she can do what she wants to me.

Last week I had this big meeting with my team. Believe it or not it was because of her. She said I made a face at her. Just because I don't care to hold conversations with her she says I have been distant.

The nurse told me she even wrote a note in my chart. But she could write until her finger falls off.

When it's my time to leave I will leave. God already has my date set to go.

I just have to keep doing what I'm doing. I can't and won't allow anyone to take what God has given me.

This is my joy. Yes, I hate it here but I have to make the best of it at the moment. I have my family who loves me and most of all I have God Almighty. Sweetheart, I will tell you this time and time again. Don't worry, be happy. If you're feeling down, pray.

Another thing, you can read a book. You can write, do puzzles, I couldn't believe it when I put a 1000-piece puzzle together all by myself.

Summer is coming so when you're home keep your mind occupied. That's what I do while I'm here.

Sweetie, when I was in jail for one year and 8 months I was in a small cell locked in 23 hours a day. I had to read, pray, do word search puzzles – anything to keep myself busy. Praise God I made it through. Has anyone told you they love you today? Mommy loves you! ☺

I'm ending my letter but never my love for you ☺

Love, Mommy

Many hugs and kisses

12 January 2003

Dear Nikki,

May peace and blessings be upon you and the family. I pray by the time you receive this letter you're in great spirits. As for me I'm holding on thanks be to God. Sweetheart you have me feeling mixed emotions.

When you didn't hear from me you tell me that you were worried. Then when I call you, you don't have very much to say. I would think that being that you don't see me and I'm away you would have endless conversation for me.

But it's all right, sweetheart, I'm all right with it. You just let me know how often you want to hear from me. Once a week – is that enough for you to hear from me? You don't ever have to worry about me. Mommy will always be all right. I love and depend on God. God gives me the strength I need to make it through whatever comes my way. I love you so much my precious angel. I can't wait for the day that this will all be over but it will be in God's time. He doesn't come when we want him to but he always comes on time.

Sweetheart I'm ending this letter but never my love for you.

Love your mommy

Many hugs and kisses ☺

19 March 2003

Dearest Nikki,

My Precious Angel, do me a favour. When people are pushing your buttons walk away. I have learned so much while being here at this hospital.

We have been learning something called RET which stands for Rational Emotional Therapy. In that class it teaches you that you get yourself mad.

I want you to think about that. People you can't control but you can control yourself. I want you to hold it together and be a peacemaker.

You and Roland have such bad tempers. But my being here has changed me slightly. I guess you had to learn how to fight. Well anyway, my precious, remember that God is love. Don't allow people to make you do things you don't want to do. I pray I am home with you soon so we can go to church together.

Let your education stay focused. Pray. Pray. Pray. Read your children's bible. You are not supposed to be fighting. Getting your beautiful face all scratched up.

Please if it can be avoided do avoid fighting. I know you have lots of anger inside but pray to God or write about what is bothering you. It's bedtime, my Angel, so I am going to say goodnight and sweet dreams.

Mommy loves you and misses you so much!

30 June 2004

Dearest Nikki,

How is my angel?

I have tried to call you on a few occasions. I am glad you are out there enjoying your summer. You stay strong and no matter what always remember that I love you. Baby Girl, please stay a little girl as long as you can. Stay away from those nasty boys. They will tell you whatever they think you want to hear to get what they want. If you ask me they are full of you-know-what.

Well I guess there are some good guys out there.

But sweetie I want you to stay away from them for now. You have your whole life ahead of you. You have to get your education and make something of your life. I want you to be a young woman who can take care of herself.

I don't want you to be with a man because you need him. I want you to be with him because you want to be with him. You go to work and make your own money. I don't want you depending on anybody.

You be an independent woman. That is where I made my mistakes. I never had a steady job and I got involved with men that were no good. I want the best for you. I don't want you to make the same mistakes I made in my life... Man will fail you every time. God is always a prayer away. Continue to pray every night. Baby, it is about time to get out of here. I just wanted to write to you and let you know that I am always thinking about you. Okay Precious I am ending my letter but never my love for you.

Love, Mommy

Homemade birthday card November 2004

Nikki, we have a special kind of communication that needs few words and little time, a rare understanding that has grown strong enough over the years to weather long silences and distant partings, and still continues to grow.

(inside) You and I are best friends and, in some way, will always be together. You are such a blessing in my life. Thank you so much for loving me and not giving up on me. I love and miss you. Love Mommy

Accompanying letter:

God is going to make sure that we are forever happy. All the things we lost we will have back. We may not be able to see your brother and sister until we are in heaven but we know we love them now and always will.

We have to accept the things we cannot change. We cannot allow our past to determine our future. Tomorrow is not promised to us. We must learn to take life one day at a time. I want you to never let anyone say anything to upset you about your mother. You have seen me.

I am the healthiest I have been all my life. This is why I look so young. I am being moulded into the person that God wants me to be. I promise this is all for a reason.

God willing, I will be a psychologist. I will be Dr Roberson until I get married then I'll add my husband's name maybe.

All right, baby, this is all for now. Has anyone told you they love you today? Well God loves you! And your mommy loves you more than words can express.

Many hugs and kisses, Mommy

I never wrote back.

It's not like I didn't want to – I just didn't know what to say. I could never find the right words. Just once I succeeded in writing a one-page letter but it came back to me because I used the wrong postage. After that I gave up trying completely.

I thought she would be content with the occasional phone call but looking back I wish I'd tried harder. Mom stopped writing to me after a couple of years – I guess there wasn't much point since I didn't write back to her. She still sent cards at birthdays and Christmas but we confined our communication to the once a week phone calls and that was it. I wish she still wrote to me now. I miss those bouncy, happy letters of hers, so full of hope and prayers and love.

The fact was, I was a very mixed-up little girl. I'd take up a pen and my hand would hover over the paper, fixed and frozen in mid-air until eventually I'd put it down again, racking my brains to think of something to write. Finally, exhausted, frustrated and my mind completely blank, I'd give up.

Because the truth was too painful to write down and everything else seemed trivial and pointless.

I was angry, hurt and confused.

I wanted to scream at her: *Why did you leave me? Why did you kill my brother and sister? Why did you get messed up with all those drugs and men and bad things? Weren't we enough for you? Didn't you love us enough?*

She talked of blessings and peace and how our lives would be so good now, but my life wasn't good, it was a mess. And I blamed her.

The trouble was – I wasn't ready to tell her that.

I wanted to be her Precious Angel still, her Baby Girl, her special friend and the wonderful daughter she painted me as in the letters. Each day I got a letter, I'd run to my room, throw myself on the bed and devour every word, line by line, slowly savouring the delicious outpourings of love and affection that came from her hand. I'd been starved of my mother's love for so long, it was food and drink to me. It was everything that I needed and once that had started, I was terrified of doing or saying something to make it stop.

In the letters I could believe that she loved me as much as she claimed and that all the wonderful plans she outlined were just around the corner. I needed that so badly that I pushed the tiny, nagging doubts about her imminent release to the back of my mind, refusing to recall what I'd read in the newspaper reports about my mom being too dangerous for release.

So I did as she told me – I prayed hard for her freedom. I wanted her to get out so that she and Grandma could pick me up and take me to her favourite restaurant. I wanted Mom to get back to the real world where she was going to study to become a psychologist.

Because I needed her in the real world.

Outside of the hospital, life was hard – I struggled to bond with my family, had a difficult time keeping up in school and found it hard to stay on the right path.

Mom's answer was always the same: pray pray pray! Not bad advice when I think about it now but it seemed so trite at the time, so easy for her to say.

How successfully had she managed her own life when she was in control? Taking her advice was sometimes a bitter pill to swallow, especially when the reason for my difficulties was down to her in the first place.

*

Of course, I soon realised that all this talk of the beautiful life we were due to share together was probably never going to happen.

Milestones came and went and Mom failed to gain her freedom.

I had to get my first bra at 12 – my grandma took me.

And then I started my period. I didn't tell anyone – not even Theresa. One morning I noticed some blood spots on my pyjamas and I knew it must be my period. So I sneaked some pads from Theresa's bathroom and took them to school with me. Fiddling around in the school toilets, I managed to teach myself how to attach the sticky bit to my knickers. And later that day I went to see the school nurse to get another batch of pads.

These were all things I should have done with my mom. If she'd been there I would have told her immediately but as it was I was too embarrassed to talk to Theresa about it.

I was growing up, but silently, furtively, behind everyone's backs.

Meanwhile, Mom talked about how the years were flying by and how God had blessed our family. It certainly didn't feel like it to me but instead of contradicting her, I just didn't reply.

Over time I started to see patterns emerging from Mom's letters and calls – she could be fine for a few weeks but then she might call and say something really strange like: 'You know your Grandma's having twins.'

I'd let it go, careful not to shatter her illusions: 'Oh really? I hadn't noticed.' Then I'd change the subject. The next time we'd speak her voice would be slurring and she'd be talking really slow.

I came to realise that Mom wasn't cured or her 'old self', she was just the same as before. Underneath it all there was still something very wrong with her mind but now, in the safe environment of the hospital, her behaviour could be controlled.

Whenever she went through a difficult patch, they just upped her meds and that's when she'd end up slow and zombified.

She'd complain about the staff in the hospital but I knew that they were only doing their jobs.

After the first year, I stopped praying for her unconditional freedom. It didn't seem right. Instead I asked God to help her come out at the right time and no sooner. I asked God to make her better first.

How could I ask God to set her free when I knew her mind was still in turmoil? Look what she'd done the last time!

We never talked about Mellie and Momo – at least, she never brought them up. Occasionally I mentioned their names but she never raised the subject herself.

One time on the phone I told her about a dream I'd had about them.

We talked for a little while and then she paused before she asked: 'Do you have any anger towards me?'

I didn't know what to say.

In the silence, she went on, 'Because, you know, your brother Roland has a lot of anger towards me. Do you feel angry too?'

'I'm not like Roland,' was all I could manage.

'Well, how do you feel about me?' she asked. 'Can you tell me how you feel?'

The short answer was no, I couldn't tell her, because I didn't know myself. I had a whole lot of stuff going on at that time and to ask me to put it into words was asking the impossible.

So I fudged it.

'I love you, Mom,' I said. 'And I really miss you.'

And that was true – it was all true.

The trouble was I was living with the memories of the past, haunted by ghosts on my very doorstep.

Our old house in Amityville, 501 Broadway, wasn't far from where we lived, right across the street from the fish market.

Occasionally, Theresa took us there when she had to buy tilapia.

I'd stand on the street corner, staring up at the apartment where Mom had lived with Mellie and Momo, recalling the years before when she'd be at the window, clutching her Bible, her mouth silently working the words of the Lord's Prayer.

At that moment, I'd be drawn back in time to when I was seven, watching my mom going mad, not knowing what was happening or how to stop it.

Sometimes my imagination was so vivid, I could see her standing right where she used to stand, in the window.

And then, through a hazy fog, I'd hear my name being called over and over again. Finally I'd feel a gentle hand on my shoulder and come out of my wakeful dream to see Theresa standing over me, a concerned look on her face.

I must have zoned out but I wasn't aware of it.

Over and over I told myself that it was meant to be, that it was God's will that Mellie and Momo should be angels. Because I knew that had they lived, their lives would have been terrible. I knew what we went through as young children and couldn't imagine a lifetime of that sort of treatment – alive, they would have been miserable. But it didn't stop me missing them every single day.

'It's the small things you miss,' Mom would tell me over the phone.

'Just being able to open a door, for example. You

know I haven't opened a door for myself in years. Or a window. Sometimes I'd just like to throw open the widows and get some air in here. But I can't.'

In my world, the problem was reversed. I had to open all the doors myself, nobody was here to help me. I knew Theresa loved me, and in time, I allowed myself to love her back, but it wasn't the same as having my mom there.

When I was sick with chickenpox Theresa cared for me like her own daughter – I couldn't have asked for more. The poor woman had accepted her husband's love child into her life and made room in her heart for me. But I wanted my mom.

14

Mixed Up

I WAS 13 the second time I tried to run away.

I went to school and called my uncle Jerome from a payphone.

'You better come and get me,' I told him firmly, 'cos if you don't I'm just gonna take off and go some place where no one can find me. I don't care what you say, I'm not going back to that house today or any other day.'

I'd had enough of my dad – his unpredictable mood swings, coldness and the simmering threat of violence. All I wanted was to be reunited with my grandma – why was that so impossible for everyone to understand? Why did they insist I stay with my father if I was so unhappy? I just couldn't work it out.

'Well, where do you want to go?' Jerome asked.

'Take me to my grandma's,' I replied in a flash.

'I can't do that, Nikki – you know I can't. Your dad doesn't want you over there.'

'Well, you better come and get me because I'm not going home.'

So that afternoon Uncle Jerome picked me up from school. Grandma was in the car with him and at first my heart soared but then I saw the route he was taking wasn't to her house but back to Amityville. We were headed straight home again.

And guess who was there waiting for me – my dad!

I ran to my room, hurt and hysterical by the betrayal.

My uncle's girlfriend Aunt Melissa was there too and my crying sparked off a huge row in the family and at some point, somebody called the cops. As soon as they came in the house, they took me into my room on my own and sat me down on the bed.

'What's wrong, Nikkia?' the cop asked me.

'I don't want to stay here,' I sobbed. 'I want to live with my grandma.'

'Well, why don't you want to stay here?'

'Because I'm scared and if y'all leave me here I'm going to kill myself because I don't want to be here!'

I meant it at the time – I know it sounds dramatic but I didn't want to go on living under his roof. Being dead, at least I'd be reunited with Mellie and Momo. At least I'd have them.

The effect my words had on the police was immediate and decisive. They put me in the back of the car and took me down the precinct.

At first I was scared – I wondered where they were taking me and why we were going down to the station instead of my grandma's house. By this point I was really tired and all I wanted was to curl up and fall asleep in Grandma's lap while she stroked my hair.

Once we got to the police station they took me to a small white room with padded walls. I'd never heard of a padded cell before but I instantly understood what it meant – if I wanted to kill myself, they weren't going to provide me with any means to do it.

For the first time in my life, I made the connection between my mom's mental state and my own. It hit me like a smack in the face – my God, maybe I was mad too! Was this the first step on the path she'd taken? Everyone said I looked just like her; what if I was like her in every way?

I sat down on a bench attached to the wall, my mind racing at a million miles an hour, my breathing short and shallow. What would become of me if they thought I was crazy like my mom? I didn't want to be locked up; I cherished my freedom.

It's just that I didn't want to live in my dad's house. Maybe I wasn't mad, I was just very unhappy. Could being miserable make you mad?

As these questions chased themselves round my head, the door of the cell opened and closed as a troop of kindly, well-meaning people popped in for a 'chat'. They asked me a lot of questions about what was going on in the house – was my dad beating me? Was he touching me?

I was scared – I didn't want them to think I was mad

and lock me up and at the same time I didn't want to get my dad into trouble. It didn't occur to me to lie so I just told the truth and hoped they'd see I was still sane.

'He doesn't beat me or touch me,' I admitted. 'But he beats my brothers and sister.'

After several hours of this one of the original cops who came to the house walked in and sat down next to me. 'You're getting ready to go home now,' he said kindly.

And at that point, I still had hope. I really thought I'd got through to them and finally somebody was taking my wishes into account.

I got up to follow him out but then I saw my dad standing in the reception area and my heart sank. I was going to go back to his house again. I was too exhausted by this time to even weep or protest. I'd done and said everything I could think of without telling a lie and still nobody listened.

It was very late by the time they let me out the police station – close to midnight – and we had a horrible ride home. My dad didn't say a thing to me, just drove through the empty streets, staring straight ahead, his face set and grim. I fell asleep on the way back and when we arrived he slammed the car door to wake me up. I raised myself and followed him into the house.

After my second attempt to run away I was made to take therapy by social services. I went a few times and I got asked the same questions over and over again: How are you feeling today? What's going through your head? What's on your mind?

It was okay but all I really wanted was to live with my grandma and it seemed crazy to me that everyone was making such an effort to keep me at my dad's house when they could have done something to help me properly and sent me to live with Grandma.

I didn't tell them I still had thoughts of killing myself – I didn't see the point. It got me nowhere last time and in some ways, I enjoyed keeping these thoughts to myself. They were my comfort, my private consolation.

It's okay, I'd tell myself. *If things ever get too bad you can kill yourself and be with Mellie and Momo again.* That was my exit strategy and I think, in some ways, it kept me sane. After a while the therapy stopped and nobody at home mentioned my attempts to abscond.

My visits to Mom were few – once or twice a year at most. My dad refused to take me because it was too far away so I could only go when I was with my grandma, and my visits to her were limited too.

When I did see my mom, we played Uno and Solitaire and laughed and had fun. I knew she loved me – she never failed to tell me so all the time – but I couldn't help remembering the way things had been when she was on the outside, when the drugs and men had come first. She'd drop us at Grandma's house 'for the day' and then not come back. Grandma would be calling and calling but she wouldn't answer the phone. Sometimes we'd be left for two or three days – how could she love her kids when she was doing that?

One day, during one of our phone calls, I decided to ask her what I wanted to know.

Mom was being concerned, asking me if I was okay, if there was anything she could do to help, if there was anything I wanted to ask her.

When she asked me that I paused for a second or two, then I said, 'Tell me, Mom, did you know what you were doing that day?'

There was a sharp intake of breath on the other end of the line, followed by a heavy silence. My heart was in my mouth. I just wanted to know the truth from her – I wanted answers. If she loved Mellie and Momo, how could she have hurt them so bad?

'Mom?' I asked, hesitantly.

Then a low moan erupted from the other end of the line: 'No, no, no! I didn't know. I didn't know what I was doing. I still don't – they tell me what I did but I can't believe it. I don't remember anything. I loved you all!'

She was now crying and screaming at the same time.

I didn't know what to do so I tried to soothe her, like a parent calming down a toddler on the brink of a tantrum: 'It's okay, Mom – it's okay. I know you love us.

It's okay, honestly. Don't think about it. Come on, let's talk about something else.'

I didn't want to hear her upset or crying. I didn't want to be the cause of that so I changed the subject. After that I didn't want to ask Mom any more questions.

So I asked Grandma instead.

15

Grandma

'ARE YOU SURE you want to know, Munchikin?' Grandma held my hand and looked at me searchingly across the dining table. 'I mean, it ain't very nice and I'm sure it's going to upset you – God knows, I don't like to think about that day myself very often. I can't. Not without all that pain coming back.'

I'd chosen a rainy Saturday afternoon to talk to my grandma – it had been playing on my mind so much recently and I felt consumed by questions about what happened that day in June 1998. I told her how I'd read the reports on the internet about what happened that day and the case afterwards. I knew it was her who had found my brother and sister.

'I have to know what happened to them.' I shook my head. 'I feel like they want me to know. You were there. You saw them. Please, just tell me what you saw.'

Grandma sucked in her breath and rearranged her skirts thoughtfully. I could tell she was weighing up whether to share with me the recollections that burdened her every waking hour. I was still only 13 after all – but Grandma had always shared stuff with me and I knew the time was right. I was strong enough and I needed to know.

'Please, Grandma,' I begged. 'They're my brother and sister. This is so important to me.'

She looked at me again. 'Well, if you think you going to be okay and not get nightmares, then I guess you have a right to know,' she said.

'I'm strong enough,' I said, then added, 'I won't get nightmares, I promise.'

So, she started to tell the story...

'Well, okay. As you know, I speak to your mom every day. I know that the weekend before we were all in Brooklyn and she been acting crazy then but I'd seen her worse than that so I didn't think there was anything really wrong.

So then the week goes on and it's a Thursday and there's this real bad thunderstorm and I talk to your mom on the phone in the daytime and she says that lightning is hitting on her stove like drums! She says it's like lightning coming into her house. So I gets to worrying about if she's doing them drugs again.

You know, your mom had been through rehab to get off those devil drugs and she was doing really well. She been clean six months already and I was proud of her. I seen her every Sunday and she was straight as a die.

So when I hear her talking like this, I ask her straight out. I says: "Are you doing anything you ain't got no business doing?"

You know, I'm concerned.

But she says: "Oh no! No – I don't do drugs no more."

"Well, God's trying to tell you something," I say.

"Well, I ain't doing no drugs, that's for sure," she says again.

But you know, when God comes up like that, you don't see Him but He trying to tell you something!

We left it alone like that.

Later that night she calls me at ten o'clock – we're talking, talking normal but in the background I can hear the baby. Sonny's crying – so I asks her: "What's wrong with Sonny?"

"I don't know what's wrong with Sonny," she says. "He's been crying like this all day."

"Why?"

"I don't know, he's just been crying like this."

We put the phone down and I feel something is wrong – the storm is over and the house is very quiet.

At 11 p.m. she calls me back. She says: "You know, my kids they been sleeping for a very long time. I went to check them – I think they dead."

Just calm, normal like that.

I says, "What do you mean?"

And then she hangs up.

Oh my God, I run down the stairs and I get Jerome. I

say: "Jerome, we got to go to Amityville cos Debra says she thinks the kids are dead."

And I'm scared as hell because I get a feeling there's something really wrong in that house. So Jerome drives us to Broadway and we run out of the car and go up the steps but when we first get there we can't get in the house because she has the door locked.

I call out her name over and over and I hammer on the door like crazy but she don't answer and I can't hear no sounds coming from inside the house.

Now I'm really fearing for those kids.

So Uncle Jerome crosses the road, which is real busy, to get to the payphone in the garage opposite the house and he calls the cops. When they get there I tell them what she said and they call out to her and knock a couple of times before they decide to break down the door.

The cops go in first and they shout for me to stay where I am but I can't help myself, I want to know they're okay so I rush in after them and I can see she's standing in the middle of the floor in a puddle of urine and her face is purple. Purple!

She's standing there in a trance and I'm screaming her name over and over but she doesn't react.

I see that she's standing over Sonny and he's on the bed and I think – thank God, he's still alive. I can see he's okay.

But the whole house is soaked – there's water all over

the dark wood walls and everything has been demolished, turned upside down. It looks like a dumpster in
there – and your mom's just standing in the middle of
the floor with her eyes rolling back in her head.

The cops say to me: "You stay here." They don't want
me coming round the apartment with them but I don't
listen to them.

I walk behind them and when they look in the
bedroom I look at the same time – and that's when I see
them on the couch.

Mellie is lying on Momo's lap and they have big blis-
ters on them. Momo has a blow on her forehead, like
she's been hit by a heavy object. I know they're dead by
the way they look – they're swollen. Their heads are as
big as adult heads and you can see, they been dead a
long time.

And that's when I faint.

The next thing I'm waking up in hospital and I'm
hysterical and I can't believe what I've seen.

Later your uncle Jerome tells me that after I faint the
cops take Debra and they throw her on the bed and put
her in handcuffs.

Jerome says to them: "You don't have to be treating
her that bad."

You know, she had wet herself but they don't let her
change her clothes and that's it, they take her out of the
house barefoot.

You know, they locked your momma up in a jail for

a long time before she was put into the hospital but no one knows what happened that day. Your momma don't remember.

The autopsy said Mellie died from scalding but not Momo, she had a big blow on her forehead, right in the centre, like she had three eyes. So she got hit with something, we don't know what. There was a big pot on the stove and the cops say that's what your momma used to boil up the water to throw round the apartment. She did it again and again and again – must have, because I saw that place was soaking wet.

I didn't know what to think – I couldn't imagine your momma ever doing something like that because I know one thing, she loved your little brother and sister. But you know what her lawyer told me? He says that at the spur of the moment, she didn't see Momo and Mellie, she just saw fire and the devil.

You know, she'd been doing drugs. They found some left over in the house.

She lied to me – I thought she was clean but she was doing drugs for a while. She told me later that she got crack from this guy and when he came in, he did it first and he flipped out.

And I asked her: "Why on earth would you take any when you saw that?"

She said: "I don't know why I did it."

But she did and she lost it too. And then she was unconscious and coming in and out for a long time that day until Sonny's crying woke her up. Maybe that's when she came back to herself and called me.

The lawyer says that when someone is on crack it's not the same person – she had no idea what she was doing. It could have happened in a minute and she won't know she's even done it.

The day of the funeral – I felt light as a feather. Honey, I don't know what the funeral home gave me, this teeny tiny white pill made me feel so relaxed. I remember you sitting on my lap but I don't remember much else that day.

Your grandpa and I stayed in the house for a month after that – we felt so bad, hurting so much. We didn't want to face any peoples.

We all had to get on medication – even me! And I'm the big bad one. I lasted a long time before I took them but you know I was shaking like a leaf on a tree. I was so nervous and jumpy. I was on them for a year and a half. Like you, I had so many questions but no answers.

They wouldn't let me see your mom for a long time but I spoke to the police and her lawyer. I says to them: "I want to ask y'all one question. You keep saying my grandkids died with hot water. Does my daughter have any burns on her body?"

The answer was no. So I says, "Well, how could my daughter do this if she didn't get burned by a little bit of water?"

And they says, "That's a very good question."

But they don't give me an answer.

So your mom pleads not guilty by reason of mental defect and she goes off to Mid-Hudson and I go to bed every night and I see them two babies.

And every day I wake up and I see them again, lying on the couch. Not a day passes when I don't see them. Your uncle Jerome is the same because he saw them too. He says that whoever did that to them should rot in hell, even if it was his own sister.

I ask God – I ask Him if there's anything I done wrong to make this happen and he says no. But I still see those kids.

And now your momma is rotting in that hospital and there ain't a damn thing I can do about that either.'

Grandma stopped talking and clamped her lips together, eyes gazing out into the distance. I could see the anger and the incomprehension in her face – I could see the questions behind her words and the many sleepless nights lost to the horror of what she saw.

She stayed like that for a few seconds before shaking her head, pushing herself up to her feet and clearing up the plates on the table.

'So now you know, honey – and maybe it's going to help you but I doubt it. Because I can't tell you anything you don't know already from those newspaper reports. All I can say is that there is a terrible tragedy, our own tragedy, and we all gonna have to live with it for the rest of our lives.'

Things didn't change that much after Grandma told me what she saw – my brother and sister's death remained a mystery and at the heart of that mystery was my mom.

I still had the same dreams, the same terrible nightmare where I was being chased by someone with a gun. I couldn't see who was behind me and I didn't know who they were but I knew if I didn't run fast, they would kill me. So I ran and ran, my mouth dry, my heart thumping, overtaken by a fear so all-consuming that I'd wake up to find I was sweating and crying in real life. My face would be wet and for hours afterwards I'd still feel that same terrible, paralysing terror as if I was still in the dream.

I had that nightmare pretty much every week – but more than that I dreamed about my brother and sister. Just ordinary things like playing together in the house or having a tea party. I was so happy when I was dreaming I'd wake up and the crashing realisation that they weren't here with me was enough to put me in a terrible mood all day.

I carried a lot of guilt back then. I was convinced that if I'd been there, I could have done something, I could have saved one or both of them. Whenever I told someone that they always said that I wouldn't have stood a chance – she would have killed all three of us.

But I didn't think so. At least I would have called the cops or gone outside and found help.

Not a day went by when I didn't think about Mellie and Momo – they were with me always. And the worst thing was that I couldn't think about them without imagining the terror they went through that week and the pain they suffered on the day they died. Sometimes it came back to me when I was alone at night; other times I'd be doing a mundane task like my homework or vacuuming and I'd remember what happened.

And the same feeling of horror came over me every time.

I tried to understand it. I played it in my head so many times, sometimes from Grandma's point of view, sometimes from Momo's, Uncle Jerome's and even Mom's.

In my head I see myself as my mom, repeating the Lord's Prayer in the window, crossing myself and whispering the scriptures. Then I'm hearing voices and seeing the devil and I can see fire coming off the walls of the apartment.

He's invading my home – he's going to possess the children and destroy all of us! He's started a fire and it's creeping up the walls, great big balls of fire running up the walls to the ceiling.

Now I'm boiling the water on the stove in the big pot, watching the bubbles slowly rise to the surface, faster and faster now until the surface of the water is churning and popping and the steam is rising up like a cloud.

The flames are everywhere now, leaping off the walls, licking my body, threatening to engulf me completely.

I have to put the fire out. I must save us!

So I lift the big pot off the stove and I swing it round the flat in desperation, sending scalding water everywhere.

And I don't see them, but Mellie and Momo are standing there as I'm throwing water and swinging the pot around. Mellie gets drenched and Momo is hit with the pot. Their little bodies slump to the ground but I'm still throwing water on the walls, blinded by my lunacy, unaware of what has happened.

I boil the pot over and over.

Then I blank out.

I come to and I'm on the floor of my apartment – the kids are lying next to me. I figure they must be sleeping so I gently lift each of them to the couch and place Momo down first, in the sitting position. I lie Mellie across her lap then I pick up the crack pipe and smoke some more till I pass out.

When I wake up again the baby is crying. Grandma calls. The children are asleep on the couch...

Was this what happened?

Did she mean to hit them? Did they just get in the way?

Even as I played the scene in my head, I could hear my sister screaming. I knew how she cried and screamed. Mellie didn't scream. And he cried silently.

When Mom wrote me those letters I only ever read them once, twice at most, and then I put them away. But the printouts I got from school of the newspaper reports I reread hundreds of times. Thousands.

I was looking for clues – I couldn't lay it to rest. Every time I looked at them I wanted to see something I didn't see the last time. I want to know what happened.

I loved my mom, that was true, but sometimes just hearing her voice reminded me of my brother and sister and I'd start to cry.

Then she would cry too. I think she knew I was crying because of something she did, something she couldn't bear to remember.

16

Moving On

When I was 13 we moved house.

It wasn't long after I tried to run away and it coincided with a lot of positive changes in my life. For one thing, I loved our new home. It was much bigger than the old house in Amityville, but you know the best thing about it – it wasn't in Amityville!

I had had enough of that place. I hated passing by my mom's old house, which had become decrepit and run down over the years. Ever since my mom killed my brother and sister, it had become known as the Amityville Horror House. People were scared to go inside to look, let alone live there, so it just went to seed. Eventually they tore it down and built another one but in the years I was growing up, it stood as a permanent monument to my pain. How could I move on if I had to pass it all the time?

The house in Wyandanch used to be Nanny and PopPop's house and it was much bigger than our old place. Finally Sere and me got a proper room of our own on the front.

I had my own bed, piled high with stuffed animals, where I did my homework, a dresser with my radio and clothes and pictures of my mom and brothers and sisters on the wall. For the first time I had my own space and it felt good.

There was a large living room upstairs and downstairs, the basement was a great hang-out area. We had a pool table, wrap-around couch and bar down there. By now I was getting on brilliantly with both my half-brothers, and Sere and I were as close as I could be to anyone. I guess I felt like I was finally growing used to my new family.

I also started high school, which was a huge improvement to my life.

The high school in Wyandanch had a terrible reputation so we all kept going to Copiague High School in our old district. It wasn't strictly allowed and eventually we got caught, but for now I was really happy and settled.

High school was better than middle school in every way imaginable.

For starters, I had more freedom. We took the city bus into school instead of being dropped off and it felt so grown-up.

We could leave the school at lunchtime and go to Wendy's for burgers and after school we had to make our own way home, so we could spend time at the end of the day hanging out with friends.

The cafeteria was bigger, the food was better, the choices were brilliant and in my classes there were kids of all ages, which I liked a lot.

I flourished in high school. I became a flag girl and I had my first boyfriend.

It started in the summer of my first year – as a flag girl we had to train at camp over the summer and Anthony was on the football team so he was there too.

I'd given up the clarinet after middle school because I loved to dance, just like my mom, and the flag girls were a formation team that paraded and marched for the school, twirling and throwing flags in the air and dancing.

The key was to make different patterns or formations in time to the marching band. The drums would be lined up on one side and the clarinets on the other and we'd be in the middle, spinning our flags in formation. The flags were big – five feet long – so you had to be really strong just to hold them up, let alone spin them. We had to do special arm exercises to get strong enough.

Our main job came at half-time during the football matches, providing the main entertainment for the crowds. We competed with other schools in the district and our team was the best in the area, so if we wanted to stay in the team we had to work damn hard. And it was tricky enough just to throw the thing up in the air without letting it land on your head! I practised for hours and hours and hours.

At camp, I noticed Anthony almost straight away – he was good-looking, like the rapper Fabulous, tall and dark-skinned. We exchanged a few looks first and then on one lunch break, he came over to my bench.

'Hey Nikkia,' he said casually, sliding into the seat next to me while I ate my lunch.

I was shy so I only just managed to reply 'Hey'.

'You been practising this morning?' he asked.

I just nodded, then he went on to tell me how the team was doing. We talked about the music we liked and as lunch was winding up he asked if he could take my number. I was thrilled – in my eyes he was one of the cutest guys in high school.

And that was it – we quickly became close.

Anthony was 17 so it was nice having a boyfriend who was older than me. I'd cut classes early and we'd go back to his house to hang out – I guess I was becoming a bit of a rebel and I loved it. Even when I got home after class Theresa and Dad were usually still at work so I could get away with so much more now that I was at high school.

At 14 I lost my virginity. My mom had warned me off boys but I liked the way they looked at me, and the way they treated me, as if I was really special. Just like my mom, I looked to them to fulfil this need I had for love. I figured that if I gave Anthony what he wanted – sex – then he'd like me even more.

Looking back now, I just wish I'd waited. It was so unromantic – his friend's car, in broad daylight on a school day, and we were parked in the school parking lot! I cringe when I think about it now!

He asked me afterwards: 'You not gonna smile or nothing?'

I flashed him a warm smile but inside I was wondering – is this it? Is this what everyone makes so much fuss about?

Still, we kept having sex because I thought it would get better as I got more practise. I treated it like one of my other extra-curricular activities – just something else I had to get good at!

One thing I was really careful about though was using contraception – I'd seen how other girls had limited their chances in life by getting pregnant at a young age. And of course I had my mom as a prime example of how teenage pregnancy could impact on the whole family so I was really careful. I still loved children and babies – in fact, I wanted to work with children all my life – I just didn't want one of my own!

So with the new house, high school and Anthony I began to feel like my world was beginning to improve. The only thing that didn't get better was my relationship with Dad.

He was still the same, mean and moody most of the time, and by then his relationship with Theresa was breaking down, which meant that he didn't come home much.

Theresa coped by burrowing herself away in her room, eating, reading and watching courtroom dramas on TV to block out the reality of their situation.

But none of us could ignore the facts – sometimes Dad showed up way after midnight and sometimes he didn't come home at all. It looked like he was up to his old tricks again – like the tricks he'd got up to with my mom that led to me.

Of course I still got into trouble – and sometimes over the most innocent things.

The one time I was seen with a boy all hell broke loose. The irony was that it wasn't even Anthony. I'd missed the bus home and a male friend offered to give me a lift. I thought I'd get into trouble if I waited another hour and a half for the next bus so I got into his car. He let me out at the end of the block as I thought it would be safer than being dropped outside my house, but just as I was getting out of the car Theresa's car turned the corner.

We locked eyes and in that moment my heart sank – it was just my luck! I knew I'd have questions to answer when I got in and sure enough, as soon as I marched in the door, she asked me who was driving – but I wouldn't tell her.

So Theresa told my dad when he came in and he put

me on punishment and threatened to beat me if I didn't tell him who had driven me home.

'You are 14!' he screamed. 'There's no way on earth you should be getting into cars with men at your age. Do you know what sort of danger you're putting yourself in? You think you know what men are like? You think you're so smart? You have no idea. NO idea at all, Nikki!'

'It's not what you think, Dad,' I lied. 'It was a girl-friend of mine. It wasn't a guy. Theresa didn't get a good look at her.'

Dad looked from me to Theresa and she shook her head, a sad smile playing on her lips. Damn! Stupid me, thinking Theresa would back me up!

Maybe she was having trouble with Dad but that didn't make her any less mad at me!

'You're lying, young lady,' he growled. 'I know when you're lying. Don't think you can get away with that kind of mouth here. I don't buy it. Theresa knows what she saw and she says it was a guy.'

He did his best to get it out of me but I refused to give him a name or point out the car the next day so I was put on punishment, which meant I was grounded for a week, no TV and reduced telephone privileges.

They were right of course – looking back now I shouldn't have got into a guy's car, but they didn't know anything about my life at the time and I resented the intrusion.

*

I never confided in Theresa or Dad about Anthony – I wouldn't dare! They thought I was trouble enough already so if they thought I was seeing older boys I would have been grounded forever!

So that side of my life stayed private – and I liked it that way.

I thought I loved Anthony – I certainly stayed with him for a while, three years in fact, but I look back now and I think I was just weak for the attention. I needed love like other people needed food – it was more important to have someone who cared for me and would wrap me in their arms than anything else.

I'd been neglected as a child, then passed from pillar to post, and I'd lost so much. So having someone to cling to, to give me love and reassurance whenever I needed it, was everything to me.

Some nights I'd tell my dad I was staying at a friend's house and instead I'd sneak out and spend the night with Anthony. Of course, in the end, he wasn't the right guy for me. I thought if I gave him sex he would love me more. I thought by being in a more physically mature, adult relationship, I would have a more adult, emotional relationship.

But in the end it didn't work. He cheated.

There were so many other nice boys around but I went for the bad boy. Don't ask me why! I think because they talk and act tough they seem strong but of course it's all an illusion. The boy I really liked but never went out with is a doctor now – and Anthony lost his mind to drugs. It's a sobering lesson and one that makes me worry I'm like my mom, always choosing the wrong men.

I still went to see Mom – my grandma used to take me on special family days. By now I was used to the drill – the security checks, lockers, long corridors and locked doors.

After the first time, the rest of the visits took place in a small cafeteria that was the patients' day room. It had high little windows running along the top of the walls and there was a soda machine and a microwave.

The one thing I never really got used to was seeing the other people in there. Mom always put on such a big smile and brave face when we visited her you'd never know there was anything wrong with her.

My mom was a simmering volcano of happiness and love – gossiping, laughing, making jokes and generally keeping our spirits up. She was always so happy and excited to see us, she'd be bubbling over with laughter, grabbing us all for hugs and kisses. Sometimes she was so excited you could see her shaking. By the way she talked and acted, you'd think everyone had made a big mistake and she was as sane as the rest of us.

But the other people in there? Well, you just didn't

know what was going to happen next. I guess that's what I found so disconcerting about visiting the hospital, the people around you were unpredictable.

One time I was there the guy next to us started banging his head real hard on the wall. He just got up and walked over to the wall and smashed it over and over again. His family was hysterical and the ward guards had to come and take him away. I felt so sorry for his family, standing there crying, not knowing what to do or what had happened.

Every time something strange happened, I felt shocked and scared.

But the worst was seeing the people whose minds had just flown away like birds. They'd sit there, with their eyes glazed over, faces completely blank, no expression, no smile, no nothing.

It was heartbreaking enough for a stranger – how devastating it must have been for their loved ones to wait months and months to see them, only to be faced with this shell of a person. Their visits didn't last long.

While I wasn't exactly the most attentive student in class, and managed to get by with only passing grades, dancing was my passion. So it was a moment of real pride when I landed a place on the cheerleading squad.

One of my best memories from that year is when Grandma came to see one of my cheerleading performances. It was right in the middle of the football game and I was so nervous and excited that Grandma was sitting in the stands I started messing up my cheer. But then I gave myself a good talking-to and completed it well – throwing and catching the pompom and cheering at the top of my lungs.

Usually, though, I had nobody there to support me. I'd get so jealous and feel so lonely seeing everyone else run up to their parents, so when Grandma came, I was so happy.

The following summer I got a job working in a café at the pool right across the street from the house and I loved it.

Earning my own money for the first time was fantastic – my freedom expanded once again and I got a real thrill out of being able to choose and buy my own clothes, food and music. Being reliant on others had always been difficult for me when they let me down so much. Now I could be independent for the first time in my life and it felt so good.

That Thanksgiving I sat round the table in our new home surrounded by all my family on my dad's side and I was genuinely really happy.

Everyone had made a dish – PopPop rustled up his special sweet potato pie, we had a massive turkey, green beans, mashed potatoes, gravy and cornbread.

Life was far from perfect but it was a darn sight better than even a year earlier – I didn't want to run away any more because I was beginning to taste freedom. It would only be a few more years before I could do what I wanted.

That night I spoke to Mom to wish her Happy Thanksgiving and for the first time I could remember I felt that things were going to be okay.

17

Goodbye, Grandma

'WHAT DO YOU mean, you're leaving?' I whispered into the receiver, trying hard to hold back the tears that were threatening to overwhelm me.

'Well, you know your grandpa is retiring next month? We figured we'd rather be down South for the rest of our years, near our families,' said Grandma slowly. I could tell she was doing her best to make this sound palatable for me but it was just about the worst news I could imagine.

My grandma was leaving to go live in Augusta, Georgia with Sonny and Roland, close to all her many brothers and sisters – a 14-hour drive from New York!

'What about me?' I choked, the tears now flowing freely down my cheeks. 'I'm your family, aren't I?'

'Of course you are, Munchikin,' she soothed. 'But you know all my brothers and sisters. They been down there waiting for us to come back someday so we can all help each other out and live a quiet life. New York ain't the same any more. We seen a nice house with a big back-yard on a quiet street. It's going to be so much better for the boys and for your grandpa. He's worked so hard, he needs a rest.'

'And who's going to be here for me?' I asked plaintively.

'Your uncle Jerome is still going to be living in New York.'

'It's not the same,' I protested. 'It's not like having you here.'

'Well, you can come for visits in the holidays. In vacation you'll be able to come stay for a long time.'

'Only if Dad lets me.'

'I'll speak to him about it,' Grandma said firmly. 'And in the new house we'll have a room for you, so that when you come you'll have your own space. There'll always be a home for you with me, honey. Please don't cry. Don't cry!'

But I could hardly hear her – I was sobbing like a baby. For the first time in my life everything had seemed so settled and peaceful. I was beginning to find my feet, to let myself enjoy life. And now the one person I trusted most in the world was leaving. I could feel my centre of gravity tilting once more as the ground shifted beneath me. For a minute I thought I would faint, so I slunk back down to the floor, my back resting against the wall, letting out a long, slow moan.

It was so important to me knowing Grandma was always there. She had been the one who'd really supported and cared for me when nobody else could be depended on. It was her I wanted to live with all along. I stayed at her house for a couple of weekends every month and we spoke on the phone most days.

When I ran away, it was always her I ran to.

Now she was running away from me – at least, that's what it felt like.

I'm sure for most people it wouldn't mean much if their grandparents moved to another state but I'd had such an unstable start in life, I depended on knowing my grandma was always there for me.

When the world was upside down and I didn't know which way to turn, she'd been the one constant I could rely on. Not any more.

It was the beginning of January when she broke the news – and she said they were due to leave mid-February.

I didn't have that long to get my head around the idea.

'What about the house?' I asked hopefully. Perhaps I could stay there? If I couldn't cling to her, then at least I could keep hold of the memories of my childhood in that house.

'We're selling it,' Grandma said. It was another devastating blow. I guess even though I knew I didn't have a choice in living with my dad, Grandma's presence in Coconut Street gave me enough reassurance to feel secure. Without her there, I felt cut adrift.

For days after she broke the news, I walked around in a daze, barely eating, unable to hold conversations, my mind always wandering during class. The few friends I confided in were sympathetic but didn't seem to understand how monumental the change was going to be. Once they'd made their sad faces and put an arm around my shoulder, they expected me to cheer up. But I couldn't be cheered.

The day they left I didn't go near their house. I couldn't bear to see the place all packed up, stripped of the furniture, pictures, dolls and toys that made it feel like home. I'd always kept a load of clothes and things at her place for when I went to visit and she promised me she'd take them with her to Georgia so she'd be ready for me when I came to see them.

Georgia! It was 800 miles away. Where would I go now if I needed to run away? I didn't have anyone to take me in.

I sat on the porch, staring into the grey, dull sky, my chin tucked into my arms, hugging my knees to my chest.

'Nikki?' I heard my dad shouting inside. He had been okay when Grandma spoke to him about me visiting over the summer vacation, but summer seemed like a million years away.

I could hear the irritation building in his voice – Jeez, the man was mad at the world these days!

'Where are you, girl?' He was stomping around the house. I could hear him slamming doors as he went room-to-room, searching for me. I couldn't be bothered to answer back. Let him find me if he wants me that badly!

'Ah there you are!' he exclaimed as he opened the front door to find me balled up on the steps, clearly pleased with himself for discovering me.

I flashed him a dark scowl.

'What are you doing out here?' he demanded.

'Nothing,' I replied defensively. 'Just sitting. Thinking.'

'Right, well think about this – there's a full trash can in the house that needs to be emptied. Can you get up off your backside and do that?'

I didn't answer. In fact, I didn't move or even look at him.

I could feel his eyes boring into me then, after a while, he raised his voice: 'Nikki? Did you hear what I said?'

'Yes, I goddamn heard!' I shouted back. He looked taken aback. I never shouted at my dad. I was usually too scared of him. But I didn't give a damn. He could do what he liked to me – beat me, put me on punishment or ground me forever. The worst was already happening – my grandma was leaving. What did it matter what he did now?

I got up and stormed past him, slamming the door in his face. I fully expected him to give me hell over that but surprisingly, nothing happened.

I didn't care one way or the other any more – it didn't seem to matter if I was good or bad, he was still mean and mad at me. So I gave up trying to make him happy.

That night I went over and over it in my head: she's gone, I kept telling myself. Grandma's gone. I just didn't understand how my grandma could leave me. How could she leave her daughter too?

We only went to see Mom three or four times a year but it was better than nothing. When I asked Grandma how Mom felt about them moving down South she was blasé.

'Oh, your mom is really happy for us,' she smiled. 'She knows that when she gets out she'll come down to Georgia and she can start her life again somewhere new, away from old, bad memories.'

It was so confusing – New York was the place I'd grown up in and all I'd known. I imagined that when Mom got out of hospital she'd come and find me and we'd live together. How were we going to do that if she was off to Georgia?

It was the middle of the school year – Grandma said they'd found a good school for Sonny but he had to restart school right in the middle of the year. Poor guy.

I'd visited Augusta in Georgia once before during a summer vacation. My grandma and grandpa took me there when I was much younger and I met a tonne of cousins. They seemed nice but it felt so far removed from my life in New York. I could barely remember what the place looked like now but I had a photo my grandma had given me of their new bungalow in the Augusta suburbs.

It looked real nice and I pinned it up on my wall that night next to my other pictures of my grandma and grandpa.

Five months, I told myself. Five months. I did some quick math in my head – that's 20 weeks until I could see Grandma again. Or 140 days or 3360 hours... That's how long I'd have until we were reunited when I went to visit in the summer.

I could wait. If there was one thing I'd learned how to do over the years it was wait.

So the months slipped by – I was still with Anthony at the time and I hung out with him, practised and performed with the flag girls and my cheerleading team and waited. Waited for the day I could go to Georgia.

We arranged that Uncle Jerome would drive me down at the beginning of July and he would take me back a week later. The long hot car journey seemed to go on for ever as we slid past mile after mile of open country. I marked off the places on the map as we passed through each town – Philadelphia, Maryland, Washington, Richmond, Newport, Raleigh, Georgetown, Columbia...

The further south we got, the hotter and stickier the air became. We peeled off layers of clothes, picked up ice-cold cherry Slurpee's from 7-Elevens and stopped off at Taco Bell and Wendy's just to get a blast of cool air conditioning every once in a while.

It wasn't just the heat that made the journey uncomfortable – I was unbearably excited and sitting still for 14 hours was simply torturous.

But with every hour that passed and every mile we put behind us, I was a little nearer to my grandma.

The first time I laid eyes on the pretty white bungalow with the neat front garden in the quiet suburb, I felt at home. They'd found such a lovely place – it was everything I imagined it would be and more. A big front porch with a couple of rocking chairs set in a pine forest glade, overlooking the evergreens. It was just right!

I nearly knocked my grandma over when she opened the door and we both wept buckets as we clung to each other.

She showed me through their beautiful white lounge to a gorgeous room with an enormous pine bed in the middle and lovely old country-style curtains and bedspread. My bedroom! It was perfect!

That night she made me macaroni cheese and green beans with chicken, my favourite, and we caught up on all the news and gossip.

Seeing everyone again felt amazing and it was especially good to see Sonny – he'd grown up so much since I'd last seen him. He was a little boy of eight now and such a funny, happy little chap. The wide open spaces and clean air were so good for him. He was getting big and strong.

'Why did you just get a bungalow?' I asked Grandma in the middle of the meal.

Their house in Coconut Street had been two storeys plus a basement and even though I loved their new home, I thought it strange there was only one level. In the city, everything was at least two or three storeys high.

'You know, honey, I ain't be getting any younger,' she laughed. 'You think I wanna be climbing up and down stairs the rest of my life? This is gonna be our last house – it's gotta be right for us for the next 20 years.'

It sounded so odd – I knew she wasn't young any more but I never imagined my grandma getting too old to move about. After all, she was still bringing up my baby brother. She still seemed so active, so full of life.

That evening we sat together on the rocking chairs on the front porch, looking out into the quiet streets as Grandma filled me in on the past few months. She'd become close to her brothers and sisters once more, joined the local church and Grandpa had started a part-time gardening business. They both seemed very content.

The neighbourhood was really quiet – it wasn't like New York where you were never far from the screech of police sirens, the thwack-thwacking of helicopters over-head or the sound of ordinary cars revving and honking their way round the city. Here you could sit out and listen to the crickets and not hear another sound the whole evening.

That night I curled up in my new bed in my new room and imagined I was staying here forever. It was further away from my mom, but it felt like a real home – a place where I could be myself. A place where I had no worries.

The rest of the week I visited all my grandma's brothers and sisters, getting to know my cousins and catching up with my brothers.

But in the blink of an eye, a week had passed and it was time to go home.

Grandma told me one of her cousins was due to go to New York the following week so I called up Dad and asked if I could stay a few more days and come back with the cousin instead of Uncle Jerome.

He didn't sound happy but after a long chat to Grandma he reluctantly agreed and I was on cloud nine!

I stayed three weeks in total, which was total bliss! I didn't want to leave at all. In the end my grandpa drove me to Maryland, halfway back to New York, where Uncle Jerome came and picked me up to take me back to Dad's house.

It was just about the most depressing day of my life

when I walked back into that place. One way or another I knew I had to find a way back to Georgia, back to my grandma.

18

Family Reunion

I LAID OUT my favourite cream turtleneck jumper over the top of my tight blue jeans on my bed then stood back to take a look – no, not quite right.

Diving back into my wardrobe, I rummaged around for another pair of trousers. It was such a mess in there! Theresa was always on at me to clear out my cupboards but I guess I was a naturally untidy person. Stuffed inside my wardrobe were old bags of clothes, school books, pompoms, flags, stuffed teddies, CDs, books – pretty much anything you could think of!

It took me a while to find but eventually I laid my hands on the pair of black jeans I was looking for. And the cowboy boots. Returning to the bed, I swapped the pants over and stood back again – yup, that looked better. I hummed absent-mindedly to myself as I picked up the jeans and wandered through to the storeroom to get the iron out of the cupboard.

It was mid-September and a Friday night – my brothers and sister were out, Theresa was in her room watching TV and Dad was still at work.

Nobody knew it but this was the night before one of the most important days of my life.

Standing up the legs of the ironing board, I casually flicked on the switch of the plug socket, placed my jeans on the board and waited for the iron to heat up.

Tomorrow, for the first time in my life, we would all be together: me, Mom and Dad.

It had taken weeks of effort and best behaviour to get Dad to agree but eventually he'd relented and said he'd take me to see Mom in Mid-Hudson Forensic Psychiatric Center.

Now that my grandma had moved to Atlanta I hadn't been to see Mom in 10 months and I think in the end my dad felt sorry for me.

When I told her on the phone earlier that week she screamed her head off – Mom hadn't had any visitors in ages.

'My goodness!' she exclaimed. 'Your dad gonna bring you up here? Well, I better make sure my hair looks good when he comes!'

Mom always asked after my dad whenever we spoke on the phone but she hadn't seen him in years – I reckon she must have liked him a hell of a lot because she was always so keen to hear news about him. Even after he'd got her pregnant and decided to stay with Theresa, she never bore a grudge against him for it.

'You don't understand!' she implored when I told her

to calm down. 'We don't see any men in here, at least not the nice-looking kind. Do you know how long it's been since I had a man pay me some attention? Your dad has always been a fine-looking man, really fine.'

I giggled. It was funny hearing her speaking like this, like a teenager about to go on her first date.

Strangely enough, Dad seemed equally on edge, maybe not excited so much as nervous.

The next morning, after I'd dressed in my newly ironed clothes, I grabbed a bowl of cereal and sat down to eat it in the kitchen. It was 7.30 a.m., early for a Saturday, and no one else was awake, but it was a two-hour drive from our home in Wyandanch to the hospital and Dad insisted we leave at 8 a.m.

Ten minutes after I sat down Dad bowled in, super fresh and spruced up! He was wearing a black silk shirt, black jacket and a pair of black pants – he'd even put a crease in the pants so they looked really good. I sniffed the air – he had on his best cologne.

Wow – he really wanted to impress her! It tickled me inside. I wanted to run over and give him a hug but he was obviously preoccupied, grabbing keys, making toast and flicking on the kettle.

He shot me a serious look. 'Okay, not long to go. You ready Nikki? I just got to check the route and then we're off. Okay?'

'Sure, Dad,' I smiled into my bowl of Froot Loops.

Ten minutes later I was climbing into Dad's red Range Rover and we drove through the quiet, early-morning streets, following a route I was by now familiar with – out of Long Island, over the George Washington Bridge, past the New Jersey Turnpike and off onto Interstate 87.

The radio was on and I stared out of the window, half-listening to the music, lost in my own thoughts until Dad spoke.

'So, what's she like?' he asked nervously. 'Your mom? Is she... er... you know, normal?'

'Yeah, she's normal,' I said. 'She's better than she used to be when she was out here.'

We looked at each other and Dad gave me a quick smile – he seemed relieved. I guess it was a big deal for him – he hadn't seen my mom since she killed my brother and sister. He had no idea what to expect – I only wish he'd taken me to see her sooner. The way he acted with Mom's side of the family, you'd think mental illness was contagious.

Maybe if he saw my mom, saw how normal she was, he wouldn't be so afraid of letting me see her and Grandma.

The rest of the journey passed in silence, the city blocks slowly giving way to wide open spaces, dark, evergreen forests rising up either side of the highway and finally leading to the entrance to the hospital.

Dad didn't seem at all intimidated by the large

collection of red-brick buildings, not like most people the first time they saw the place, but I guess since he worked in a correctional facility he knew what to expect from an institution.

We parked up, I retrieved the soda and snacks I'd brought for my mom and we walked through to the entrance.

We passed through the usual security checks, taking time to place our jewellery in a locker and were shown through to the smaller day room, not the large cafeteria where I met Mom the first tine.

The little windows along the top of the walls let in a bright stream of sunlight that bounced off the plastic tables and chairs.

As we came in we saw it was really quiet that day – just two other sets of visitors sat around, waiting for the patients to come through.

We put our things down on one of the long green tables and sat on the immoveable small round stools.

After I paid a visit to the bathroom, I emptied my rucksack onto the table and played a few hands of solitaire to pass the time while we waited for Mom to come out. After a while my legs began to shake with nervous anticipation and I found myself chewing my nails.

Dad was drumming his fingers slowly on the table, all the while his eyes darting round anxiously to see if she was coming.

Eventually I heard the familiar bang of the doors as

the patients were shown through and in a second, she was standing there.

Mom!

She looked amazing! She was dressed in a pretty pink shirt with a white hairband, blue jeans and white shoes. Her make-up was done beautifully and her long dreads flowed over the headband.

She was smiling and giggling like a little girl and I went over and gave her a great big hug. She didn't seem so tall to me any more – if anything, I was a little taller than her now and she felt small, insubstantial in my arms. She'd lost weight recently, I noted.

Dad stood up too and after me and Mom let go, she reached her arms out and they hugged. My heart was in my mouth but I didn't want to say anything. I didn't want anyone to say anything – I just wanted to stand there looking at them, making this moment last as long as possible.

I wanted to shout – it's my mom and dad! Look everyone! Look – my mom and dad are together!

It was probably one of the weirdest family reunions of all time but to me, it was beautiful.

After a while they let go of each other and I could see they were both smiling – giving each other the once-over.

Mom spoke first, her voice high and coy. 'David? How's everything? You looking good.'

We all slid into the seats at the hard tables.

'Thanks, Debra,' he smiled back, a little laugh in his voice. 'You look good too.'

'You know what – you look just the same as you always did!' Mom teased.

'You look the same too – you don't look like you aged at all.'

Jesus – they were flirting with each other! After all these years – after everything, they still liked each other!

I sat there, enraptured by their exchange, enjoying the spark between them. Inside, I was beaming. It was a really special moment, there in the psychiatric hospital, all of us together for the first time. A family.

I let myself daydream for a little while – what if it was always like this? Me, Mom and Dad together – nobody else.

They caught up on all the news, both chattering away like a pair of old friends, all the nervousness gone, Mom going on about the terrible food in the hospital, Dad talking about his family.

I didn't really speak much – I didn't have to. Instead, I just looked at their faces, wondering whom I resembled most. I wondered too if either of them knew this was our first encounter as a proper family. It didn't matter – what mattered most was just being there together.

*

After a while we each got a soda and broke out the chips and sandwiches, then I showed Mom all the photos I'd taken from my visit to Augusta.

She oohed and ahhed over the house pictures then squealed with delight when I showed her the new photos of Sonny.

'Oh my God!' she exclaimed. 'He's such a big boy now. Is he smart? He looks smart. I bet he's a smart boy. Your grandma says he does well at school. I hope he studies hard because I think that boy has a bright future.'

After a while we played the card game Spades. It's usually a four-handed game but we managed to play with three, and after we'd done with that we had a game of Monopoly.

Visiting lasts four hours so we had loads of time to relax and enjoy Mom's company – it looked like she really loved having us both there and her eyes twinkled bright with happiness.

It was about half an hour from the end and Mom was blathering away about how she loved to study the Bible and all the important lessons she was learning from the scriptures.

She usually talked to me about this when I was there and I'd half-listen and nod a lot.

'The thing is, honey,' she said. 'I wasn't ready to accept the Lord into my life when I was out. I got involved in all sorts of stuff I shouldn't have and that was the wrong path for me, which is how I ended up in here.

'Tell me, David, you still living the wild life?'

She looked up at my dad with a sweet smile on her face but he met it with a stony silence.

Suddenly he turned to me. 'Nikki, why don't you go and get a tissue to wipe up this mess here?' He pointed to the spilled soda and chip crumbs we'd left lying around the table.

'But Dad, it's my turn!' I said, waving a hand over my huge collection of properties. Mom, the Dog, was one throw of the dice from bankruptcy and Dad, the Car, had confined his buy-ups to the cheapest blue and orange properties. Playing as the Top Hat, I was a comparative tycoon! 'I've nearly got all the stations!' I objected.

But Dad wasn't in the mood to argue and his voice hardened. 'I said get us a tissue.'

It seemed strange – I wondered why he was acting like this, but I did as I was told and I retrieved a tissue from the bathroom. When I came back Mom was packing away the game and Dad was unfolding his legs from under the table.

'I'm getting a bit sleepy,' he announced. 'I'm gonna go sit in the car for the next half hour, maybe grab a nap before the drive back. Give you guys some time on your own.'

Mom got to get up as well and as he left she gave him

a warm hug and a smile – but all the happiness seemed to have left him and he gave her the briefest of hugs. I was confused and upset – what was going on? Everything had been going so well.

As soon as Dad was out of the door Mom's smile dropped and she whispered, 'He got mad at me, that's why he sent you away.'

'Why? What did you do?'

'Nothing – I jut asked him that thing about living the wild life. He thinks you don't know what he gets up to!'

'Dad doesn't like you talking to me about grown-up stuff. He doesn't like Grandma doing it either – he says it ain't right for me to be hearing about that stuff when I'm just a child. But I'm not blind, I know what's happening. He doesn't come home much. I think he's cheating again.'

Mom arched her eyebrows and gave me a knowing: 'Mmm hmm!'

It was meant to be funny and I wanted to laugh but something in the way Dad had stormed out had soured the giddy atmosphere. We both felt a little deflated.

We chatted a bit more over the next 20 minutes but when the time came to leave my mom's eyes became frantic and desperate.

She held me to her in an emotional embrace and told me again and again that I had to pray and that it was kind of my dad to bring me to see her.

'You be a good girl for your dad and stepmom, you

hear,' she ordered, her eyes darting up and down as she picked imaginary lint from my jumper. 'You be getting so big now! But remember you still a child and no matter what your dad gets up to he's still the man of the house and you need to respect that and respect him.'

I felt so sad and sorry for my mom – I could tell she regretted asking Dad the question earlier but she couldn't take it back now and she couldn't apologise to him either. He was gone.

I know how she must have felt. The way my dad made her feel – that was the way he made me feel all the time. But it was okay for him to do that to me – I was well, I was a normal person. It was cruel of him to storm out on her like this – she was on her own in this place, nothing but her thoughts and her Bible to keep her company.

When we left I just knew how hard it would hit her and how she would cry with the pain of separation from everyone and everything she loved in this world.

I loved my mom so much. In the past four years I'd come to realise that she needed love and compassion more than most people do in this world.

In the hospital she'd found a kind of peace, a balance that worked for her. She wasn't cut out for life on the outside and despite her continual prayers to be given her freedom I suspected that she feared it as much as she wished for it. And, I'm sad to say, I feared it too.

I left, as I always did, with a heavy heart.

*

Dad was waiting for me in the parking lot and I tried to hide my anger and upset from him when I climbed in the car, making my face a mask of non-expression.

But as we pulled out of the front gates I felt the tears pricking the back of my eyes. I turned away to the window, angry with myself for letting the emotions show.

Half an hour later Dad stopped at a gas station and he got out of the car to pump the gas and grab us each a sandwich.

With him in the car I'd managed to hold in my pain, but as he left I felt my whole body relax and I let the misery wash over me once more. Before I knew it I was sobbing wretchedly into my hands.

Dad opened the car door, confused. 'What's wrong with you? Why are you crying?'

I didn't want to tell him. Mom would be mad at me for betraying her confidence so I told him half the truth: 'I don't like leaving her there.'

'Well, there's nothing you can do about it – she can't come home right now. At least she gets to see you once in a while. It's better than nothing.'

I seethed inside. Did he really think that would make me feel better? Poor Mom – she'd put her faith in all the wrong people in her life. I scolded myself for my earlier fantasies of my parents getting together and us living together as a happy family. Stupid stupid stupid!

Dad couldn't be happy with anyone – and Mom, well, she didn't really stand a chance one way or another.

He wasn't the only one who didn't understand. All the kids at school just couldn't get their heads around how I could still love my mom after everything. They didn't understand that she was sick. Everyone misunderstood her.

That night, lying back on my bed, I put my favourite Jamaican songs on my headphones, the ones we used to listen to in the old house in Brentwood, and closed my eyes, letting the music wash over me and take me away to another time and another place.

In my mind, I saw us all dancing round – me, Mom, Mellie and Momo.

I was overcome by melancholy and happiness at the same time and the tears fell silently on my pillow.

Even remembering the good times was hard. I couldn't think about those snatched moments of happiness without recalling all the pain that came after them.

And once again, I cried myself to sleep.

19

Georgia

I STUCK MY head out of the window and felt the warm wind whipping back my hair as the car sped down the highway.

Freedom! For the first time in my life, I could taste freedom. And boy, was it a sweet and delicious flavour!

In a moment of sheer jubilation I shouted out: 'Yeee-ha!!!'

Uncle Jerome sat in the driving seat next to me, grinning indulgently. 'Get your head back in here, missy!' he shouted, half-joking, making a grab for my arm. 'Or you gonna lose it!'

We were back on Interstate 295 heading south out of New York, through Philadelphia, to Maryland. Another five hours and we'd pull into the McDonald's car park off the interstate where we'd agreed to meet up with Grandma and Grandpa – they were coming to get me!

In the back of the car we carried my entire life's possessions – three suitcases of clothes, books, CDs, photos and cuddly toys. It's all I had to show for my entire 16 years on this planet but I didn't care. I would have fled New York with just the clothes on my back. It was all the same to me.

It was September and I was just on the brink of starting my new life in Georgia. I was so overwhelmed with excitement and happiness I could have hugged Uncle Jerome.

Instead, I put on a fake Southern drawl.

'What d'y'all think of my accent, Uncle Jerome?' I asked playfully. 'Y'all think I gonna pass for a *jen-you-ine* Southern belle down here or you think all them Southern kids gonna find me out for me the slick-talkin' city kid from Noo Yoik?'

He laughed and I stuck my tongue out cheekily. I could hardly believe my prayers had finally been answered and after all these years of wishing and hoping, I was finally coming to live with my grandma. A new life was beckoning.

When the end had finally come for Theresa and my dad, it had been sudden, strange and chaotic.

Dad had slowly been distancing himself from the rest of the family, but when the news came that he was to be a father again to another woman that finally spelled the end for him and my stepmom.

She didn't even try and fight for him after that – I think she'd had enough and just wanted to protect herself and her future.

Then Theresa lost her job and decisions had to be

made quickly – they would divorce. Theresa would take the kids and go back and live with her mom.

My dad was due to move back in with my Nanny and PopPop and since I was under his guardianship, I was due to move back there with him too.

The idea of losing Theresa and my stepsister and brothers was devastating – but worse was the thought of being stuck on my own with Dad.

I started saving my Saturday job money and planning my escape. It would never work out with just my dad and me – anybody could see that. I had to have an alternative plan in place. I hoped I could save enough money for a Greyhound bus ride to Georgia.

Every night I prayed to God, just as my mom asked me to, asking Him to make things better.

I didn't know what on earth I expected but you know what, He must have been listening because in one fell swoop, all my prayers were answered!

One night in June after school I was in my room listening to music on my own when my dad came in. He wasn't mad, but it was unusual for him to seek me out like this. He sat down on the end of my bed. 'Nikki, can I talk to you a minute?'

'Sure,' I replied, already on my guard. Things had been so crazy recently I had no idea what to expect – as usual, I braced myself for bad news.

'Where you wanna live at?' he asked straight out.

My forehead wrinkled in confusion. I didn't know what he meant. Was he seriously asking my opinion?

'I mean, where do you want to live – here or you wanna move to Georgia?'

'Huh?' I blinked dumbly. Did I hear that correctly? Was he asking me if I wanted to live with my grandma? I felt like screaming the place down, but I managed to keep my voice under control when I replied: 'I wanna go and live in Georgia with Grandma.'

He nodded silently then sighed and looked down.

It felt like time stood still in that moment – I held my breath, anxiously awaiting his response.

'Well,' he said eventually, picking himself up off the bed. 'I'll think about it and let you know.'

And then he walked out. Oh my God – I was so excited I jumped up and down silently, my mouth agape in a silent scream.

Of course he was never going to say, 'Whatever you want darling. You can go tomorrow.' But I knew he wouldn't even have asked if he didn't intend to let me go. That night I prayed extra hard: 'Thank you! Thank you God for everything today. I know that you listened and answered my prayers. Please let Dad allow me to go live with Grandma as soon as possible!'

After that it was only a matter of time.

A week later Dad came back and said that he'd thought about things and decided it was probably best if I went to Georgia seeing as they had to sell the house to settle the divorce. As he wouldn't have a permanent home for a while he thought I'd be better off with my grandma.

I told Grandma on the phone and she was thrilled.

We were on the phone every day making plans for my arrival. I had to register at the new school in Augusta and get all my paperwork sent from my school in New York. Grandma also had to apply for residency so she could officially become my legal guardian.

Meanwhile my home and life in Wyandanch was being dismantled around me as Theresa and the other kids got ready to leave.

Every day I came home to a shifting situation as furniture got packed up and shipped off to various different places. Theresa and my dad barely spoke any more and it seemed like there was nothing left between them at all.

I wanted to feel sad for my brothers and sister but if I'm honest, I think they were more relieved than anything that their mom was finally escaping a miserable situation.

By now Sere was 17 and David was 21 and at college – Buddy was 15 but he too was taking it in his stride.

As for myself, I was torn about leaving New York.

I know it's a strange thing to say – after all, I'd wanted to join my grandma for so long – but New York was everything I'd ever known.

My mom was here – so were my brother and sister.

On the phone Mom was bubbling over with excitement for me.

'Don't you worry about me,' she reassured. 'I have the Lord with me all the time – I ain't never lonely. And you gotta be with Grandma so that when I come out I can live with you both!'

Leaving Mellie and Momo was harder – I took a bunch of yellow roses to their grave a fortnight before I was due to drive south with Uncle Jerome.

The hot summer sun beat down on the back of my neck as I bent down to lay the flowers on the parched ground.

For a moment I just squatted there in silence, uncertain what to say. Then I took my jacket off, put it on the ground and sat down on it.

'Hey you two,' I started. 'I'm sorry I haven't been to see you much recently – but I think about you all the time. You're in my heart – always.

'I'm going away soon – but I'll make sure I come back to visit. The fact is – I gotta move away. I don't want to leave you but I think this is for the best.'

The tears burned hot behind my eyes.

'At least you two got each other – take care of each other, you hear? And I'll be back to visit soon. Real soon.'

I stopped, lost in my thoughts. Where would Momo and Mellie be now if they'd lived? Fifteen and fourteen respectively, they'd probably be horribly screwed up by now. Maybe they'd have spent the rest of their childhoods in and out of care as Mom tried to hold it together.

Would they have fallen into the same traps as Mom? Taking drugs, dropping out of school; would Momo have got pregnant? Momo was a fighter – maybe she'd bet toughing it out on the streets by now, or locked up in juvenile detention. But Mellie – he was a softie – I don't think he would have stood a chance in the harsh adult world.

No, their lives would have been ruined, one way or another. I knew that.

In a way, my dad had saved me. Despite everything, all the pain and difficulties of my childhood, I knew that I was growing into a whole person. And that was down to him and Theresa.

They'd taught me discipline, responsibility, self-respect and how to follow my dreams and ambitions.

They'd kept me alive, it was true, but more than that they had given me a future – the chance of becoming a capable and fulfilled human being, someone who could be a worthwhile part of society.

I might have hated my dad, I might have been scared of him, but I was grateful too. He'd given me life lessons that would stay with me forever. Just as Mom had. In their own very different ways, they'd taught me right from wrong.

*

When the day finally came, I stood in the hallway, jumping up every five minutes to check my bags and look out on to the porch to see if Uncle Jerome had arrived.

It would be a seven-hour drive to Maryland, which meant leaving at 6 a.m.

Jerome had to make the return journey in one day and in the late summer heat he wanted to get most of the drive there done in the morning, before it got too hot.

I'd already said my goodbyes to Theresa and the kids a few days before as they'd gone to live with Beryl, Theresa's mom. I was sad to say goodbye but I knew that we would all stay in touch.

'I would have taken you, you know,' Theresa whispered as she wrapped me in her arms. 'If he'd let me, I would have taken you too.'

'I know,' I smiled, pleased she'd told me.

I loved Theresa for that. Through all these years she'd never treated me any different from the others, despite the way I'd come into her family. She loved me just as much as her own children and even when the man who was my actual father had cheated on her she was willing to take me under her wing.

When I lost Mellie and Momo, I lost the physical closeness of being near another person – Theresa gave that to me with an open heart. She hugged me, cuddled me and comforted me.

Strangely, Nanny and PopPop didn't like that – they

always said I was too affectionate with Theresa. I think what they meant was that I didn't have that same closeness with my dad. But whose fault was that? Not mine and certainly not Theresa's.

No, Theresa was a big-hearted woman. She gave me love when she didn't have to. She even gave me lunch money when my dad wasn't around. She was kind and loving from the beginning.

I squeezed her tighter then and sent up a silent prayer: 'Please God, give Theresa many blessings in this life and the next.'

We stood like that for ages then she straightened up and wiped away a few tears. 'You look after yourself, right?' she said, pulling herself together. 'Study hard, stay in school and don't go chasing after those boys.'

'Nah!' I laughed. 'Don't worry – I'm going to make you proud.'

'Good girl!'

I hugged Sere, Buddy and David – they were all crying too. We didn't say much – we didn't have to. We'd survived together and now we were all making our separate ways in the world. I told them I'd pray for them and they said they'd do the same for me.

Now I was crouching down next to my suitcase, making sure it had all my favourite photos as my dad, bleary-eyed and sleep-befuddled, emerged from his bedroom.

'He here yet?' he asked through a giant yawn. I shook

my head. I'd been up for hours already – in truth I'd barely slept the night before.

After taking a shower and making himself a hot black coffee, Dad came and stood next to me, looking out of the window as we waited for Uncle Jerome to arrive.

He didn't say anything, just put his arm around my shoulders.

I could feel the emotion welling up inside me and I knew that now was the time. Staring straight ahead, I started: 'Dad – you know, Dad, I love you. And I know that you've done so much for me.'

I paused, uncertain whether I could get through what I had to say without breaking down.

'You gave me a good start in life, Dad. I want to say thank you. For that. Thank you because I know that without your help things could have been very different for me. You and Theresa, you made it possible for me to grow up.'

I stopped – did he understand what I meant? It hadn't come out the way I'd practised it the night before. I wasn't even sure it made sense – I looked up at him and to my surprise I saw big fat tears rolling down his cheeks.

He enveloped me in a mighty bear-hug.

'I love you too, Nikki,' he sobbed. 'I've always loved you. I know you don't believe it but I've only ever tried to do my best for you. One day, you'll see. I know you think I'm a hard man but I've just tried my best to bring you and your siblings up in the best way I can.

'Just remember – I'm always here for you. If you ever want to come back, just call. You'll always have a home here.'

I wept gratefully into his arms – yes, I was excited but I was nervous too so it was good to hear Dad telling me I could come back anytime. Of course there wasn't much for me to come back to – my old home had been broken up. God knows where he'd be in six months' time! But still, it made me feel like I wasn't cutting my ties to New York completely.

Just then Jerome's blue sedan rolled down the avenue, his lights still on for the early-morning mist.

Dad pulled me away from him and stared at me hard, as if he was drinking in one last look at me, memorising every detail and contour of my face. He stroked my cheek affectionately and grinned. 'You sure are a pretty girl, Nikki!' he smiled proudly. 'Just like your mom.'

I smiled back – it felt good to hear that.

Then Uncle Jerome was at the door, and it was time to go.

20

Family History

I'D LIKE TO say that everything was great at Grandma's and I lived happily ever after. I'd like to say that, I really would.

But it just wasn't true. Of course there was so much that was great about being reunited with Grandma – but so much that wasn't. And I hadn't expected that.

I'd left her when I was a little girl and now I was coming back to live with her as a teenager. A difficult, complex, assertive young adult. I wasn't the same little Munchikin they'd known from all those years before.

In my dad's house I'd been taught to look after myself – make my own bed, do my laundry, dishes, cook, clean, everything. In Grandma's house, she did the work and everyone else just let her!

I'd been happy to let her do it too when I was visiting for a holiday but when I came to live in her house, it didn't feel right. I was independent.

Grandma would wander into my room in the morning to make my bed or clean up my room but I'd hustle her out again.

'I'm just trying to help you out,' she'd argue.

'I don't need that kind of help,' I objected, my arms folded defiantly across my chest as I blocked the doorway. 'It's *my* space, *my* room, *my responsibility*. I don't need you coddling me like a little girl!'

Each evening, after we ate dinner cooked by Grandma, I'd attempt to help out with the clearing up, taking the dishes to the sink and donning the rubber gloves. But she'd shoo me away, wouldn't let me lift a finger.

In the end we came to a compromise – the kitchen and bathrooms were my grandma's domains but I was in charge of everything in my bedroom.

Grandma wasn't overly affectionate but she was pleased I was there and she showed her love by doing things for me. Grandpa on the other hand, seemed positively put out that I'd landed in his house. Perhaps he felt he'd done enough to help me out when I'd been in New York but every time I walked into a room he frowned and walked out. In the kitchen he'd slam the cabinets around like I was an annoying fly he was trying to scare away.

When I mentioned this to my grandma she'd brush off my concerns. 'Oh, don't you pay him no mind!' she'd chide. 'He just a mean old man who don't like nobody!'

And it was true that Grandpa didn't really participate much in family life. He barely spoke to Sonny, Roland or myself and spent most of his time outdoors working on the gardens he was paid to look after.

It made me feel unwanted again – and that's a horrible feeling.

Perhaps in his mind it was all very clear-cut – you grow up; you leave home. But Grandma and Grandpa's home was always the place I imagined I belonged so coming to live with them felt right to me.

I guess my grandma and grandpa had to pick up all the pieces from my mom and maybe they resented it. They were already raising Sonny and Roland at a time in their lives when they had expected to be taking things easy.

When I arrived too maybe Grandpa thought it was one grandchild too many. But it wasn't my fault – or Sonny's or Roland's. We were the kids – we didn't ask to be born.

If Grandpa left us to our own devices, Grandma was the total opposite – she was all up in my business the whole time!

I couldn't sneeze without her telling the world I'd caught a cold!

It was a big change from my home in New York with Theresa and Dad where they'd kept a respectful distance from my private life. As long as we stayed out of their way, got our grades and behaved then they didn't pry too much into our lives.

Grandma seemed to feel that whatever went on in her home was her concern and by association, a concern for all her 11 brothers and sisters too. And their families!

I missed my period one day and the next she was on the phone blathering to all her family that I was pregnant! Of course I wasn't and I was horrified that these people who were still more or less strangers to me were gossiping about the state of my reproductive health. It drove me nuts!

And it wasn't just an adjustment coming to live in Grandma's house. I had to get used to a new school and new people. Anthony and I had broken off before the summer, so when I met Brendan in my new hometown and found in him someone who showed me the affection I craved, I clung to him. I didn't need a whole bunch of new friends, but it was important for me to just have one person I could trust and confide in. Brendan was kind and loving and exactly what I needed.

By the time I arrived in Augusta I had to start my new school too – Cross Creek High School. I didn't like it much and I found it hard to fit in. All the other students had grown up together since elementary school so they were in strong cliques. It's not like I didn't want to make new friends but I was shy and scared of getting too attached to people. It felt like everyone I loved got taken away from me at some point so I found it easier to keep myself to myself.

But more than anything living with my grandma brought to the surface all the questions I'd suppressed over the years.

While I was living with Dad and Theresa, I'd

managed to keep a lid on my thoughts about Mellie and Momo. It tortured me that I didn't know how they died but once we left Amityville for Wyandanch I'd tried to put out of my mind the questions that plagued me.

Now, living in Grandma's house, those questions crowded back into my thoughts.

Why did they have to die? Couldn't someone have done something?

Here I was, growing up in Grandma's house, just like my mom had done all those years before me and it made me wonder how my mom had turned out the way she had. What made her into the woman who killed her kids? Was there anything anybody could have done to stop it?

One night after dinner, after the boys had left the table and I was helping Grandma to clear away the plates, I asked her to tell me about my mom.

'What do you want to know, child?' she asked gently.

'Everything, Grandma! I want to know *everything* about her!'

Grandma chuckled. 'Well, that may take a bit of time.'

'I don't care,' I shrugged. 'I got time.'

Grandma sat down in front of me, her palms spread out. 'Where do I start?'

'Start with you and Grandpa,' I suggested. 'How did you and Grandpa get together?'

'Hooo-ee!' Grandma laughed. 'Now you going back quite a way!'

But she seemed pleased that I asked her about her own past and settled her skirts around her legs and sat back in her chair.

'Well, you know I had two boyfriends before I met Willie, your grandpa. But he was the one that knocked me up – as a matter of fact, he tricked me! Yes he did and I'll never forgive him for that.

We met in the April and in the June he asked me to marry him but I said no – so he found a way. Well, you know when you're young you think you're in love. So we made love and the first time we did it he used a condom but then he told me that if we did it again, I couldn't get pregnant from the second time. And you know what – I believed him!

I didn't know any better! Our parents didn't talk to us about stuff like that. It was a shock when I fell pregnant at 16.

My mother knew – she had five girls and she kept up with our periods. When it was time for it to come, she knew. That's the kind of mother I had. She came to me and she said: "Hmmm, you didn't get nothing last month."

She was mad as hell! She took me to the doctor and they told me I was pregnant and they told me the day the baby was going to be born.

And you know, your mom came right on time – 25 January 1967.

I wanted to call her Samantha but my mom chose the name Debra for her.

I was 17 when I had Debra and for a long time I was so mad at Willie, I wouldn't even talk to him! He'd come round to the house after I told him I was expecting the baby and I'd get into bed so I wouldn't have to see him. I didn't want to have a baby, not that early. I wanted to go to school. It was my mother made me talk to him and she said he would do right by me and stay with me.

"He's a good man," she said. "He's quiet, not too much to say for himself, but he's a nice man and he'll be good to you."

In the end I figured I didn't want no other man to be the father of his child. I wanted my child to know her real daddy.

Well, of all the things I can say about your grandfather I'll tell you this much: he's been a good provider to this family all his life.

We married in the July when Debra was five months old.'

'Was it easy Grandma?' I asked her.

'Was what easy, honey?'

'You know, having a baby, becoming a momma?'

Grandma let out a low whistle and shook her head. 'Noooo! No, it was not. It was scary. I was the eighth child out of 12 so I was just a baby myself. They had me spoilt rotten. I didn't know how to act. All the time I was pregnant I kept thinking to myself: "I'm gonna be a momma? Me?" I couldn't believe it.

'In 1969 we went to Indiana and then we headed to New York in 1971 when Debra was three, going on four. By then I'd had your uncle Jerome – he was born in 1969.

Your momma was a sweetheart, you know, right up until she was around 11 or 12 – then she started changing. But right the way through she was always so smart.

Debra wanted to be a paediatrician and she would get her little dolls and treat them. That was her dream and you know, she could have been that paediatrician. She was on AB honour roll right from kindergarten, always head of her class. It was always As and Bs with her. The teachers commented that she was very bright. It came naturally to her – she didn't have to work hard.

All the way through she aced; even when she was pregnant and had a baby, her grades never changed.

But her personality wasn't that great – she had a snotty little attitude. We used to get into arguments about that – I told her her attitude stinks. She wanted everything to be her way, no matter what you said or how you said it. But it couldn't work like that all the time; you have to listen but she didn't want to hear it.

At 11 she started getting with boys and she got pregnant at 14. I took her to get the abortion. She didn't want to be pregnant – she didn't even know what she had done. I put her on birth control pills but she wouldn't take them.

She got pregnant again at 15. And I took her to get an abortion again – but this time she got very, very sick. She got so sick I thought she was gonna die and I said: "Next time you gonna have that baby."

And that's how Roland came along because I refused to take her to get another abortion when she got pregnant at 16. Whether she wanted that baby or not, I didn't care. I couldn't face losing her.

So Roland was born and I had to look after him while she finished high school. The teacher even came to the house and taught her at home for six weeks when she had Roland, then she went back to class.

So from the beginning Roland was always like my baby. Debra needed her sleep at night to do her studies so I took the responsibility of taking care of him at night.

Then she got her own apartment and she went to school to be a court stenographer. She had six more months to go for that and she was getting good grades and then she met up with that Beanie! And that's when everything went down the drain.'

I'd been listening intently when suddenly it struck me that Grandma had missed out something vitally important – me!

'What about my dad?' I interrupted.

'Mmm hmmm,' Grandma nodded. 'David! Yes, Debra thought your dad was going to be her husband. She was in love with David. He took her to his house and he told her: "This is the house we gonna be living in!"

'And she thought that was the truth. But then he went and married Theresa. That really hurt her – that's when she started going backwards.

I don't know – she wasn't very smart when it came to men. I mean, David had already been with Theresa a long time and they had two children together. When she got together with him she couldn't see that he was already taken. Nope, she went right ahead and had a baby with him – you! I told her: "You don't need to have a baby with every man you meet!" But she didn't want to listen to me – she thought that was the way to keep a man. Well, Theresa had two children by David and neither of them little ones stopped the man from straying! She couldn't see the reality of the situation. I always felt that she was looking for love in the wrong areas – your grandpa, you know he was a great provider, he installed phones into big buildings and that made our lives very comfortable but maybe he didn't show his love to his kids so much.

Anyway, David broke her heart and that's when she married Beanie – she didn't love him at all. I could see that but she didn't admit it to me at the time. Only later she told me she fooled herself into believing Beanie was David.

And it was Beanie got her on drugs – not that I knew anything about that at the time. I was real naïve – I didn't know about the drugs for years.

After she got married she had Mellie and Momo and that's when your mom and I were arguing really badly. I got angry with her cos she kept on having babies. But now her argument was: "Oh well, now I'm married so I can have as many babies as I like."

Well, as you know, Beanie gave her two babies and walked away. It didn't make no difference that they was married.

And that's when everything started going wrong.

She was around 28 the first time I took her to the psychiatric ward. She was seeing things that weren't there and saying all kinds of crazy stuff like: "My kids are possessed by the devil. My kids must die because they possessed."

I took her into the hospital and at first the doctors didn't want to tell me what was wrong but I said to them: "You better tell me what's up with her because she acting crazy. I don't care if she grown up, this is my child. Tell me what's wrong with my child!"

Eventually they said it was a bad dose of heroin.

And I was like: "Drugs? My daughter don't do no drugs!"

I was arguing with them! I couldn't believe it because

she had kept everything so smooth, I never would have known but this bad heroin sent her crazy and it was a real bad shock.

They kept her in for two weeks and when she came out they had her on antipsychotic medication.

After that first time I asked her why she started taking drugs – she couldn't answer me. She didn't know herself, only now she couldn't stop.

So a pattern started up – she would be fine for a while then she'd stop taking her medicine, she'd get on the drugs again and she'd end up back in hospital.

Next occasion it was the same thing, she'd stop taking her medicine, start talking crazy, she would get the Bible and just read the Bible over and over again, real loud, and that's how I knew she was going back to that stage again.

She never wanted to go to hospital but I knew she had to. I took her to the psychiatric hospital five times in total.

Every time she swore to me when she came out that she'd stop doing the drugs and keep taking her medication but she lied to me about that over and over again.'

Grandma paused for a moment to take a sip of water, shaking her head as if to dispel the bad memories.

Then she looked up, her eyes full of tears.

*

'It's when she started doing crack that things got really bad. She forgot about all you kids completely – she was just strung out on that stuff so much.

She would drop y'all off at five in the afternoon and come back at midnight. I was doing too much, trying to work as well and it was so stressful.

I didn't know what was going on or what to do.

Meanwhile, you was growing up into a sweetheart – so loving and soft-hearted. You always loved babies – and your mom took advantage of that. You looked after your little brother and sister as your mom got more and more taken up with her drug life.

Then you got molested and after that I found out about you kids getting left on your own and I took you away to try and force her to look after her own babies – I tried everything to make her be a better mother but nothing worked.'

'Why just me?' I asked her bluntly.

'Hmmm?' My grandma looked confused.

'Why did you just take me away from Mom? Why didn't you take all of us?'

Grandma folded her arms. 'After you were born I told your mom I wasn't going to be taking care of no more of her children. I wanted to stop her having more kids. I was run ragged! I couldn't take it! I was already bringing up Roland so when I told her I wasn't going to take care of any more I meant it! In the end the CPS took her kids away while she was going through rehab but after she got her place in Amityville they gave them back.'

'But Grandma – if she was on drugs all the time, don't you think it would have been better to take Mellie and Momo too?'

'Of course!' Grandma snapped. 'I know that now! But at the time I wasn't thinking like that. I never thought for one minute your mom would hurt you or any of the others. She always loved her kids.'

'And she was always lying to me – when she said she was clean, she was doing drugs!

The thing was – I felt I could help you. You was in school – I wanted to make sure you had a stable home life and not run from pillar to post all through the night going to different places.

Also, I wanted her to take care of these two children and maybe that would stop her from having any more babies. But it didn't. She had Sonny afterwards by a new guy.

I found out later both him and Mellie were born addicted to drugs.

By then your dad was back on the scene and he said he wanted to take custody of you and I thought it was probably for the best because he had a solid home life. On the day they went for the custody hearing your mom never even showed up to court.'

*

Never even showed up to court? My mom just gave up on me without a fight. That hurt really bad but I didn't break down. I had asked for the truth and now I was getting it. No point stopping now. I had to ask her – it had tormented me in the dark hours of the night.

'What about that day in Brooklyn, Grandma?'

'What day, sweetie?'

'You know – the Sunday before Mom killed Mellie and Momo. We all went to Brooklyn together. Do you remember? Mom was acting real crazy.'

I had to know – I had to find out what happened that day and why nobody stopped my crazy, drug-addicted mom from taking two innocent lives.

'Yeah, I remember that day,' my grandma said warily.

'Tell me what you remember, Grandma,' I urged. 'I want to know.'

'Well, I remember Debra was acting silly that day, reading the Bible again. She was acting off the wall. I think she had stopped taking her medicine. I don't know if she was on drugs.

It was raining and she stayed outside under the tree with you kids.

I don't know why she didn't want to come inside. It was raining real hard and I said: "Fine, you stay in the rain!"

So we brought the kids in the house and then she

finally came inside. It was raining very hard. I remember stopping her from taking you when she wanted to get you all on the subway.'

'She was screaming at people and kicking down doors,' I interjected. 'Do you remember that?'

'No,' Grandma said slowly, shaking her head. 'I didn't see that. Anyway, she calmed down after a while and came inside. Later on we dropped her back home with Sonny, Mellie and Momo and went about our business. By then she seemed like she was okay again.

I remember your grandpa asked me that night: "Do you think those kids safe with her the way she is right now?" I said I thought so, but I didn't know.

And that was it – I was tired.'

Grandma stopped speaking and looked at me expectantly.

'Didn't you think she was doing crazy stuff, Grandma?' I asked her hesitantly.

'Not particularly, no,' she replied.

I couldn't believe what I was hearing. 'Really? Standing outside with us kids in the rain, making us recite the Lord's Prayer on our knees in the park? You don't think that was crazy?'

'You gotta understand,' Grandma responded. 'I'd seen her much worse than that. One time she was so crazy he turned up every bottle in the house and emptied perfume on your head! I came home from work to find her at the top of the stairs pouring out water from the sink.

'One time she threatened to cut my head off with a knife! Another time she demolished my home. No, I don't think she was that bad that day. I'd seen her worse. All she wanted to do was read her Bible. I asked her if she had taken her medication and she said yes but she was lying.

I didn't think those children were in any danger, of course I didn't! Don't you think I would have taken them if I thought for a minute she would harm them? Don't you think I ask myself that too? Now it's me who wakes up every day with that image in my mind of them as they were lying there, their swollen heads as big as melons. I see that every single day.

And your momma is locked up and maybe she'll never get out! They tell me she's bipolar but I never heard of bipolar before. I reckon it was the devil, the devil made her take them evil drugs and that was it!'

Our conversation was over – Grandma got up from the table, her hands shaking, face red and her little hands balled into tight fists.

I didn't want to see her like this, I certainly didn't want to be the cause of it – but it was important for me to hear what she had to say.

I sat back in my chair and sighed. I had a lot to think about.

21

Reflections

WHO KILLED MELLIE and Momo?

I lay in bed staring up at the ceiling, the question repeating over and over in my head.

Was it the devil, like Grandma said? Was it my momma? Or was it this bipolar illness?

After we'd talked that night I found myself going back over what she told me again and again. My brothers had been born addicted to crack. My mom had been admitted to a psychiatric hospital five times in the three years before she killed them. There were incidents with knives, alarming and erratic behaviour and a complete disregard for the welfare of her own children.

Couldn't anyone see she was dangerous?

It struck me as completely unbelievable that no one from CPS or my family had stepped in to do something. Grandma was naïve, it was true, but she wasn't dumb. She said herself that Debra 'wasn't right' – anyone with eyes and ears could have seen that!

*

For months after our conversation I found myself at loggerheads with Grandma – it was always over petty little things like coming home late or missing dinner but behind it all was my difficulty with what she had told me that night.

I just couldn't come to terms with her explanation of the events leading up to Mellie and Momo's deaths.

She knew her daughter was ill. If anyone knew then she did – she took her to hospital enough times! Why didn't she do something? Or Grandpa, for that matter?

Even if they didn't have the ability to take Mellie, Momo and Sonny themselves, they could have called CPS and had them taken into care. Grandpa even asked Grandma that night whether she thought the kids were all right with Mom. They must have seen she was unstable.

Gradually it dawned on me that there was no way Grandma would have wilfully ignored the facts. Like she said, if she'd thought for a moment that my mom was going to hurt any of us, she would have done something.

So why couldn't she see the danger?

Perhaps, when it came to my mom, Grandma suffered a blind spot. After all, she was all ready to blame Beanie or the devil or CPS for what my mom did. She even blamed Grandpa to some extent! She said Debra turned out the way she did because he never gave my mom enough love when she was growing up so she went looking for it elsewhere. Never once did I hear her say: 'It was Debra, my daughter. She did it. She's to blame.'

She even started spouting theories about there being another person in the apartment when Mellie and Momo died – maybe that was the person who killed the children! It was ridiculous – Mom had already pleaded not guilty by reason of mental defect.

Grandma had an excuse for everything. 'The lawyer convinced her to plead that way,' she told me. 'But the police never investigated the crime scene properly.'

'Grandma! Mom did it! You know she did,' I'd argue back.

But Grandma shook her head stubbornly. 'I don't know nothing. Maybe it was somebody else.'

It was in turns infuriating, baffling and depressing.

According to Grandma, Mom was never responsible.

Her attitude made me look around at what was happening at home with Sonny and Roland – they never had to do anything for themselves or take responsibility. If either of them ever got into trouble Grandma always pointed the finger elsewhere. They never got punished, never felt the consequences of their actions.

Had it been the same with Mom?

As the months passed I became more and more unhappy living with Grandma and Grandpa. The arguments between us got worse – they were never about my mom, just the day-to-day frictions of life. But underneath I found it difficult to accept Grandma's reasons for letting Debra keep the other children.

After a year I went to live with my boyfriend Brendan – and started working in Taco Bell to help pay my way. It was a relief for all of us.

Free from Grandma's constant scrutiny, our relationship improved and I felt able once again to show her the love I felt for her. I'd always wanted to live with my grandma but by the time my wishes were granted it was too late. I was already my own person making my way in the world. I had my own dreams, my own wounds and my own battles to fight. Grandma couldn't live my life for me.

I kept up at school, despite falling behind with my grades, worked hard and visited my grandparents and brothers once a week.

And right then, just when I wasn't looking for them, the answers that I'd been looking for all my life landed at my feet.

It was a Sunday early in December 2008 and I was round at Grandma's house. I'd turned 17 the month before and bought my first car. It was a bit of a wreck but I loved it and I was so thrilled to finally have my independence.

I'd driven round to Grandma's house for Sunday lunch and we were chatting in the kitchen.

'Something came in the post this week about your

mom,' she said casually. 'You might want to take a look.'

I opened the anonymous brown envelope and inside was a sheaf of A4 pages stapled together – the title on the front sheet read: Relapse Prevention Plan and underneath was my mom's name.

'Am I allowed to see this?' I asked my grandma, uncertain about the nature of the privacy surrounding my mom's condition. Grandma had no such concerns.

'I don't see why not,' she shrugged. 'I'm her legal guardian so it's really up to me and you're her daughter. If your mom ever gets out I think it's important you should know about this.'

I took the pages in my hand and started to read.

The purpose of this plan is to identify information I may need to maintain psychiatric stability and avoid circumstances which may lead to violent behaviours. It is important that my Relapse Prevention Plan include very specific information so that it will be useful in a variety of situations and settings.

Diagnosis – Schizoaffective Bipolar Type

This is caused by a chemical imbalance in the brain. When I am ill, I suffer with psychosis and mood disorders at the same time. When I am symptomatic, I become delusional by believing that I have healing powers. I also believe that the verses in the Bible refer to me and I am supposed to do what I interpret from reading the scriptures in the Bible. I have bipolar symptoms in which my mood swings are happy and then sad. In addition, when I am sad I isolate myself from people. However, when I am happy I have a lot of energy and I do not believe that I need much sleep. This is why it is important that I take my medication for the rest of my life.

I was open-mouthed with amazement. Grandma had alluded to the fact that my mom was bipolar, but until I read the report I didn't fully grasp what that meant. From what I understood the drugs she'd taken had driven her crazy. But that's not what it was saying here – it was describing an actual mental illness. For the first time it struck me that I'd got something very fundamentally wrong in my understanding of what happened to my mom.

I read on. Below the diagnosis was a list titled 'My Specific Symptoms':

1. Delusions: Thinking everyone were devils.
2. Insomnia: Not sleeping for days.
3. Paranoia: Thinking everyone is out to kill me.
4. Anger: Cursing people out and calling them names
5. Impulsivity: Throwing water on children.
6. Poor judgement: Thinking the children were possessed.

7. Healing: Putting children underwater thinking I can heal them.

8. Fear: Afraid of everything and everyone around me.

9. Racing thoughts: My mind thinking constantly about irrational thoughts.

10. Isolation: I did not want to be around anyone.

11. Preoccupation with the Bible: Reading the Bible too much and thinking it is referring to me. Thinking I am supposed to do what it says.

The next section went on to list a whole host of medications my mom was currently taking and after that there was a section titled 'Early Warning Signs'. These listed all the signs that my mom was about to have a relapse like not taking her medication, becoming aggressive, reading the Bible too much and being suspicious of people. Next, it listed some triggers and risk factors – one of them was titled 'Birthday of Children in Heaven'.

The next few pages listed ways to avoid a relapse like staying away from drugs and alcohol, keeping appointments with doctors and reporting early warning signs. Number one on this list read: 'I understand that I need to take my medication for the rest of my life.'

After that there were various other lists about what to do in a crisis and who to contact. Finally there was a plan for my mother's eventual release – it said she would be sent to live in a civil hospital and after that a community residence and finally a supported apartment.

*

I don't know how long I was sitting there reading the plan before I heard my brother Sonny come in to get a drink.

I hurriedly shoved the papers in my bag – Sonny was 10 years old now. He didn't know what had happened to our mom, he was still too young.

But reading this document, things suddenly started to fall into place for me.

I think for the first time in my life it was clear to me that my mom wasn't mad, bad or possessed by the devil – she was sick.

I flicked back to the list of drugs again – there were six different drugs listed here including antipsychotics and mood stabilisers. They were necessary because my mom had a chemical imbalance in her brain. It wasn't her fault, or Grandma's, Beanie's or anyone else's – she had been born with this illness and now she needed to be on medication for the rest of her life.

All the anger I'd held on to suddenly melted away – I couldn't be mad at her any more. I didn't have a choice – I had to forgive her.

I went to sit on Grandma's porch by myself to be alone and let the information slowly sink in. All those times when we were younger and she acted crazy – that was the illness. Those times I didn't know what mood she was going to be or how she was going to act – that was the illness.

Later on I looked up the condition on the internet and familiarised myself with what it meant. The bipolar part was a mood disorder – it meant my mom's moods were extreme and needed to be controlled with medication.

The schizoaffective part meant she had hallucinations and delusions in every sense – she could hear, see, smell and taste things that weren't there.

These hallucinations would worsen if the person was intoxicated and sometimes the person could experience delusions like they had a special purpose or destiny in life.

It all fitted so well with my mom – it was a perfect description of her. The delusions, the racing thoughts, the paranoia and the anger. And it wasn't her fault.

But with that realisation came a second, not-so-comforting thought – if my mom was ill, did it mean I would inherit her condition?

Looking at the list of symptoms I knew I experienced some of these myself – I'd had racing thoughts before and fear of other people. At times I didn't feel comfortable around other people at all, even when I knew them really well. I knew that wasn't right. When I got really stressed out I would feel my mind start to race with worries about how I was going to pay my bills and get by in life. I'd get really depressed, then I'd start to have suicidal thoughts, telling myself I didn't want to be here any more, it's too much. I can't deal with it.

I could usually get a handle on things after a while really by giving myself a good talking-to! I'd tell myself that things weren't as bad as they seemed. I'd give myself a pep talk. But was this normal? Did everyone go through this?

Now I worried for my mental health – and that in itself was depressing!

I did some more research online and found that although by no means conclusive there was evidence to suggest that schizoaffective disorder could be passed on to children. In other words, if you had one parent with the condition, you stood more of a chance of being affected than most of the rest of the population.

I started to analyse my mood swings – I could go from being really nice and softly spoken to angry in a second. People knew me as a calm, shy girl but when I was angry, I could be a monster, I knew that. Even as a pre-teen I got into fully fledged fights with other girls – before now I'd always put it down to my tough upbringing on the streets, my natural defences kicking in. Survival.

Now I wondered whether there was something more sinister at work.

I certainly had my bouts of depression too, times when I just needed to lie down in a quiet place on my own without being disturbed. Those were the times it felt like the walls of my existence were crumbling in around me and I had to do everything in my power to hold on to my heart and soul.

But I didn't drink and I didn't do drugs – in truth I was terrified of losing control completely and after a few boozy experiments I found drink only made life harder for me, not easier.

So there were definitely mood swings – but were they abnormal? I was still a teenager! We were supposed to be moody, right? I don't remember ever hallucinating or being delusional but then how would you know if you'd hallucinated? The point was you were meant to believe that things from your imagination were real – so what would distinguish a hallucination from an ordinary experience?

In the quiet, early hours of the morning I'd lie awake, mulling these things over in my mind.

I knew I looked like my mom, I'd inherited a lot from her, but this too?

I didn't know the answer to that and I'd have to wait another year before I came any closer to finding out.

22

Graduation

'SMILE!' SERE ORDERED as I clutched my diploma in the square outside the James Brown Arena, and for about the millionth time that day I pulled back my lips and grinned like an idiot!

My face hurt from smiling so much but it was a good feeling.

Standing there in my floor-length gold and burgundy gown, my mortarboard perched awkwardly on my head, I felt so happy and proud.

I looked around at all my high school classmates, surrounded by their friends and family, and for the first time in ages I felt I belonged, I felt like everyone else.

In truth, I never believed I would graduate from high school.

By the time I left New York I was already well behind with my studies and the disruption of moving to another state didn't help.

Under Dad and Theresa's strict control, I'd been forced to knuckle down and study hard but as soon as their household began to break up, they became distracted and I guess my thoughts were elsewhere too.

I moved to Georgia as an eleventh grader but already I had to repeat some classes from the year before. It still wasn't enough so Grandma paid for me to go to summer school the following year. She was determined that I was going to graduate.

Unfortunately I didn't have enough credits to complete the year.

When I realised I'd failed math and social studies and would have to return to high school, I felt utterly despondent.

I felt that I'd always been running to catch everyone else up. I'd had to work extra hard when it came so easy for many others. Was I just the Dumb Dog I'd been called all those years before? Maybe I just wasn't bright enough to make it through high school? In that respect, I wasn't like my mom one bit. By all accounts it seems she sailed through all her exams without any trouble.

Other people were smart, not me. I was good with kids and caring and all that but when it came to academic work, perhaps I just wasn't cut out for it.

Already I'd forced myself through two years of a high school I hated and I was impatient to start my life properly.

I'd got a job working weekends at Taco Bell and during the week I worked at a local day care, which I loved.

'Maybe I can get my GED?' I suggested to my grandma one evening as we discussed my future. A GED was an equivalency certificate similar to a high school diploma.

'Don't be ridiculous!' she exclaimed angrily. 'Them GEDs ain't worth the same as a diploma. If you want to be a nurse, you'll never make it with a GED.'

It was true. All my life I'd dreamed of being a maternity nurse, one that works with newborn babies in hospital. Without a high school diploma my chances of getting into college to study nursing were very slim. But I just didn't think I could do it.

'Tcha!' I tutted, shaking my head. 'I've been at school a long time already and I'm done with it.'

But Grandma wasn't in the mood to argue: 'No you ain't! You done when you got that diploma in your hand and not before!'

Over that summer Grandma kept up a relentless campaign to convince me to stay in school and if it weren't for her I don't think I would have gone back. I have her to thank for keeping on at me and making me stick to my studies.

Sere was also a great help – she was in college studying accountancy by then and she talked to me about school a lot and encouraged me to stay. And Theresa was also there for me, making sure I was confident enough to stay on course.

'Don't you listen to what anybody else tells you,' she

told me over the phone from New York. 'You're a bright girl and you deserve a bright future. I know better than anyone. I brought you up. If you weren't smart, I wouldn't be telling you to stick at it!'

Theresa had gone to college herself and worked in medical coding. She knew that if I wanted to achieve my dreams I had to graduate and get into college.

Added to all that my mom called me every week on the phone and did her very best to boost my confidence and invest me with the excitement about studying that she felt she always lacked.

'Don't you do what I did,' she chided. 'Don't take your education for granted. You've got a chance here, Nikki, to make something good of your life and I know you're smart enough to take that chance.'

Somewhere over that summer, with all their combined help, I found my motivation again and by the following September I was back in school five mornings a week, working hard to catch up on my credits.

The rest of the week I had a job working with kids in day care and any spare time left over was given to study.

It was a tough year. I hated the humiliation of returning to the same classes I'd flunked just 12 months before – but I did it and on 24 May 2009, I found myself standing next to all the other kids who were graduating, grinning from ear to ear! It felt really good.

*

That morning I'd woken up to a full house. Theresa and Sere were staying with Brendan and me in the house that we had together. They had come all the way down from New York just to see me graduate! Sadly my dad decided not to come but I didn't mind – I had lots of family supporting me that day, including Grandma, Grandpa, Roland and Sonny. Another cousin was graduating too so by the time we met up at the James Brown Arena in Downtown Augusta with all the family, we were a large group of dozens of aunts and uncles.

I was wearing a new outfit I'd bought for the occasion – a white polka dot skirt with a black halter-neck top, black tights and heels.

Grandma had helped me buy the $50 gown and mortarboard three months before and the day before the ceremony, she got it out and ironed it for me.

'You look really cool,' Sonny smiled up at me as I awkwardly hoiked the strange gown around my shoulders. Was it meant to keep slipping down like this? My gown was so long it practically touched the ground – it was just as well I was wearing heels!

'Thanks,' I replied, nervously looking around at the hundreds of teachers, students and their families gathered at the front of the arena. I was glad Sonny could see me like this – we'd grown closer over the past few months and I wanted to be a good role model for him.

Brendan looked at his watch: 'Come on,' he said. 'It's getting on for two o'clock, we'd better go inside.'

There were so many people, I started to get scared. Crowds always made me feel uneasy. We went into the large stadium and my family found their seats while I was ushered to the front, in one of many rows of chairs designated for graduating students.

Looking round the massive stadium, I tried to locate my family but it was so cavernous and full of people I couldn't see where they were. I suddenly felt very lost and alone and a quiet panic began to build inside me. Then my eyes alighted on my cousin, who was seated in the row in front of me and waving at me like a maniac. It was a relief to see a familiar face and my heart began to slow a little as my breathing returned to normal.

The rows were arranged in squares and after the hubbub had died down and everyone had found their seats, the start of the ceremony was announced.

The principal gave a short speech about how graduation formed an important basis for a lifetime of learning, then two rows per square were called to come to the front to accept their diplomas.

I watched as one line after another got up noisily and made their way to the front, each student making the long journey across the stage to the principal's hand for a quick shake before exiting off to the other side to have their photo taken.

There were around 200 of us graduating that day so it took a long time, but eventually my row was called to the front.

We walked down the centre aisle to the sounds of clapping and cheering.

Oh God, I sent up a silent prayer, *please don't let me trip up as I'm going up the stairs!*

My lengthy gown kept slipping off my shoulders and getting caught up in my black heels. I was terrified I was going to fall over and make a complete fool of myself so I gingerly climbed the steps, lifting the sides of my gown and watching my feet intently.

Each step was torturous – like scaling the side of a mountain – and at one point I felt my heel slipping into the back of the gown but I quickly hitched it up again and managed to avoid disaster.

Phew! When I got to the top of the stairs I felt over-whelming relief just at having made it this far without landing up flat on my face!

My cousin was right behind me and we grinned nervously at each other as we stood side by side on the stage, waiting for our names to be called.

Then I heard someone say: 'Nikkia Roberson' and somewhere from deep in the dark auditorium a tremendous noise erupted as my whole family started yelling and screaming.

I couldn't help smiling as I went over to the principal to receive my diploma – it felt amazing. I know it was just a small piece of paper but I'd worked so darn hard to get it! It was the key to my future – the chance to achieve everything I dreamt of in life. A chance for happiness and fulfilment.

As I took my diploma I knew there were two others with me by my side, my beloved brother and sister Mellie and Momo. At that moment they were both there with me, accepting my diploma, experiencing this monumental milestone in my life. And I was proud that they could both share it through me, because they were never going to experience it for themselves.

Afterwards we were ushered out of the doors of the auditorium and a whole bunch of students threw their hats up in the air but I didn't want to throw mine – I didn't want to lose it!

I was keeping this gown and mortarboard for the rest of my life!

My cousin and I had only been outside a few minutes before we were enveloped by my family, who covered us both in hugs and kisses. Cards and balloons were pressed into my hands, I got dizzy hearing everyone say: 'Smile Nikkia!' and my jaw started to ache from the non-stop grinning.

'I'm so proud of you,' Grandma whispered, her eyes shining with tears.

'Thanks Grandma,' I gave her a giant bear-hug. 'I'm proud of me too.'

At that moment Grandma clapped her hands to summon everyone's attention.

'Right, folks,' she called out. 'I think we had enough pictures – let's get ourselves some food!'

We all crammed back into our cars and drove off to Ryan's Buffet where I piled my plate high with everything I could find including macaroni cheese, string beans, fried fish, French fries and pizza. I didn't hold back! I even managed some ice cream and fruit at the end of my meal, despite being stuffed to the gills!

Then in the dappled late afternoon sunshine we drove back home – I was taking Sere out on the town that night so we had to go back to my place to shower and get ready.

We were in the middle of doing our make-up and hair when my cell phone rang.

Finally! This was the call I'd been waiting for all day long!

I picked up the phone, all excited: 'Hello?'

There was a pause and then down the line, in a clear and tuneful voice, my mom sang to me: 'Happy graduation day to you! Happy graduation day to you! Happy graduation day my dear Nikkia! Happy graduation day to you!'

I was giggling and laughing as she held the note far too long then let off a series of whoops and cheers which must have sounded really noisy in the hospital!

I was so pleased my mom had called to congratulate me. All through the day, I'd been thinking of her. As wonderful as it was to have so many members of my family there supporting me, I missed her so much.

By then we'd been apart for 12 years but there were times like this when it was so hard to be without her. I would have given anything to have her by my side.

I had looked around at all the other happy graduates being primped and preened by their proud mothers that day and couldn't help feeling saddened by my mom's absence.

But now at least she was here on the phone, congratulating me and even singing to me! I told her all about what happened that day and when I'd finished there was a long silence.

'I would have liked to be there too,' she said at last.

'Yeah, Mom,' I sighed. 'I think you would have liked it.'

'Well, you know I was thinking about you the whole time,' she said. 'And I sent you a card. You know, I'm so proud of you, Nikki. I know it ain't been easy for you.

'Now you make the best of your life and get yourself to college so you can get a good job and make your own money. Don't you be like your silly momma!

'I don't want you being with a man because you need him. I want you to be with him because you want to be with him. You go to work and make your own money and don't be depending on nobody else.

'I'm counting on you to do all those things you say you're going to do. It's your life now, honey, and you've got to make the best of things.'

'Thanks, Mom,' I said, tears of gratitude springing to my eyes. I needed this – I know it might sound strange but I needed my mom giving me these little pep talks. That's what made me feel normal again.

'Listen, I have to go,' she said. 'Go out and have a good time tonight with Sere. Just look after yourself out there!'

Now it was my turn to lapse into silence. There was so much I wanted to say but I didn't know how. So much I wanted to share with her but couldn't.

'I'm thinking about you too, Mom,' I said eventually. 'And I'm coming to see you real soon.'

'Ok, baby,' she said. 'Come see me soon. But don't forget – I'm always here for you, even if it's only on the phone. And God is only a prayer away.'

'Okay, Mom. I love you.'

'I love you too – with all my heart.'

23

Mom Again

Two months later and I was striding down the long, bright corridors of Mid-Hudson Psychiatric Center once more, my heels making a smart clipping sound on the white linoleum flooring.

'Jeez, Nikki, slow down will you?' Sere called out behind me in exasperation. 'You're not going to be late you know!'

I stopped for a moment.

'Sorry, sorry,' I mumbled. 'I'm just real excited. That's all. It's been too long.'

'I know,' Sere laughed. 'But seriously – you gotta slow down for the people with the little legs!'

I laughed, probably too loudly, probably too hard. I didn't care.

It had been three years since I'd last seen my mom and I was bursting with anticipation. Sere was putting me up in her college house for a couple of weeks over the summer vacation and she'd agreed to make the long drive out to the Hamptons to see my mom with me.

'Are you sure you wanna go?' I asked nervously the night before. She'd never met Mom when she was in her right state of mind, or been to a psychiatric hospital for that matter. 'You really don't have to do this, you know.'

'I wanna meet your momma!' she insisted. 'After all these years, don't you think I'm a little curious? She's important to you so she's important to me too. And don't you think she'll be disappointed if I don't show up?'

God, she was right! Mom didn't get very many visitors now that most of her family had moved down South. She was so thrilled when I told her I was coming to visit with my sister.

'Oh bless her!' she'd breathed down the phone. 'What a wonderful treat! You truly have a beautiful sister. You've been so lucky, Nikki. Never forget that. Tell your sister I'm really thrilled to be meeting her.'

Now the day had finally come and I couldn't be held back. It was all I could do to stop myself from running towards the day room.

We settled ourselves into a corner table and I started to unpack my bag – we'd brought all sorts of goodies for my mom this time – pizza, soda and tonnes of photos of the family in the South and my graduation day. There was so much I wanted to share and show her in my new life.

We didn't have to wait long – after ten minutes the patients came marching down the corridor, all in a long line, just like the first time I'd come to visit.

I spotted her immediately – she'd grown her hair out into long dreadlocks that she'd dyed a honey-gold colour reflecting a radiant glow from her skin. The happiness seemed to shine out of her!

I sighed in admiration. She looked magnificent!

After all these years she was a fine-looking woman, just like my dad said, and she was obviously looking after herself because her skin was shimmering, her teeth were all pearly white and she was slim as a teenager!

We fell into each other's arms in sheer, exuberant joy and for the first time since she had been locked up, I felt all my heart letting go when she squeezed me hard.

Knowing what I now knew about my mom, and her illness, I felt nothing but love and forgiveness for her – I felt healed.

The previous month of June had been a tough one – it always was since it wasn't just Mellie and Momo's birthdays but the date of their deaths too. During that month, she'd called me frequently, upset and agitated. 'The staff here are horrible to me!' she'd complained. 'They're restricting my Bible reading time. It ain't right. I want it investigated!'

I listened sympathetically and did as I was told when she ordered me to take down their names and numbers.

A few days later she called back, her voice languid and slurred from being doped up on medication. I knew they'd had to sedate her because she was too emotional.

'You okay, hon?' she drawled.

'Yeah, Mom, I'm okay,' I assured her. 'Don't worry about me. Just remember I'm coming to see you next month. Remember that!'

So I tried to keep her buoyant and after the anniversary of the deaths on 24 June her dark mood lifted and she began to recover her stability again. By the time of our arrival she was back to her old self – funny, bubbly and mischievous as hell!

'I've got a boyfriend,' she whispered conspiratorially when I commented on how well she was looking.

'Mom!' I laughed, bemused. 'How do you manage to have a boyfriend in here? Ain't they got rules for that sort of thing?'

'Shhhhh!' she frowned, motioning with her hands for me to keep my voice quiet and sneaking looks at the staff keeping watch from the sidelines.

'He works here. I'm not meant to have a boyfriend! But he likes me and I think he's cute. We go into the storeroom because he's got the key and we kiss! Sometimes he lets me touch his thing!'

At that I roared with laughter! Sere too was giggling uncontrollably.

'You don't understand!' Mom was looking at us both earnestly. 'I haven't touched a guy in 12 years. I sure as hell missed it!'

And I'd missed my mom – nobody talked so frankly to me. It was true that Mom wasn't like normal people – she was direct, surprising and always entertaining.

We talked about Georgia and the family and she asked Sere lots of questions about her life. The two of them got on so well I wished I'd taken Sere to see her earlier.

Mom devoured all the pictures we'd brought then we cracked out the pizza and enjoyed a mini-celebration.

'To my daughter!' Mom held up her soda in the air as if proposing a toast. 'Who was smart enough to stay in school and graduate, even when things were tough. To my little girl who's making it in the world on her own!'

Sere and I looked at each other and I grinned.

'To Nikkia!' Sere echoed.

'To me!' I laughed.

Afterwards we played Yahtzee and then Monopoly. I was just scooping up the dice for my throw when my mom grabbed my hands.

'Gosh, look at that!' she exclaimed.

'What?' I replied.

'Your hands! They're exactly the same as mine.'

Mom was turning my hands over in her own.

'You've got the same wrinkly fingers as me,' she laughed. 'And look, the same thumb that bends backwards!'

She was staring down at my hands, examining them in every detail when it struck me that nobody had ever done that before, just held my hands and looked at them so intently. And staring at my hands in hers, I saw she was right. They were practically identical.

I smiled – my mom and I were connected. I belonged to her.

It was true I was out there in the world alone, but sitting here with her in the psychiatric hospital, I didn't feel quite so isolated.

There was somebody I belonged to. Somebody like me.

I held on to her hands tightly then and gave them a big squeeze.

We were bound together by a bond nothing and nobody could shake, despite all the time and distance that passed. Despite everything that had happened. People could say what they liked, think what they liked, it didn't bother me. She was my mom, the only one I was ever going to have and I loved her no matter what.

Mom and me still speak on the phone every week and she still sends me letters and cards. I hope one day she'll be able to join us in Augusta but I know that realistically that day might still be a long way off.

On the whole I know that the hospital is a good place for her – while she is there she seems to be in her right mind for longer periods than when she is on the outside.

There are times she still says things that don't make sense, like when she tells me that my grandma is expecting twins or that somebody is after her. If she's anxious then she'll try and pray with me over the phone and I can tell from her fast and jittery delivery when she's on the brink of a manic episode.

The real giveaway is her laugh – when she's herself, her laugh is beautiful, relaxed and natural like a waterfall. When she's uptight it's high-pitched and forced.

Those are the times I'll sit with her on the phone and try to calm her down, let her know that I still need her. Just because she's inside and I'm on the outside, it doesn't mean I need her any less. I still ask her advice and seek her views because she's incredibly wise and clever.

When she's unwell, I tell her I love her as much as I can and just wait until she's recovered. She's never aware when the illness starts to take over and I don't point it out. Why would I? It wouldn't help her.

I'm pleased to say that my mom seems happy. In hospital she feels safe and she doesn't have anything to worry about. She sees things going on in the world and it scares her. As much as she wants to get out, I think part of her is frightened of the real world. It has been so long, it would take a lot of adjustment for her to operate on the outside.

After all, her life is much simpler in the hospital. She doesn't have any bills to pay, appointments to keep or jobs to do. Everything is regulated from the time that she gets up to the food, drink and medications she takes.

I don't envy that – I wouldn't trade my freedom for the world – but sometimes she doesn't understand how difficult life can be for me.

For instance, if I tell her my job doesn't pay well enough to cover my bills she tells me to get another job. Yes, well it's easier said than done!

I think maybe if my mom was stable for a whole year she might be ready to come out. Sometimes, when they've given her a lot of medication, I ask her why they did that and she never tells me it's because she's flipped out, she never admits that to me.

It doesn't matter. That's for her to come to terms with, not me.

I forgave my mom a long time ago for what she did but that doesn't stop me wondering what happened to Mellie and Momo on the night they died.

I hope one day my mom remembers so I can lay their ghosts to rest. I think that perhaps somewhere, locked in her unconscious, is a memory too awful for her to face right now.

It wouldn't make any difference to my relationship with my mom – as far as I'm concerned we will always share an unbreakable bond – but I can't deny that I'm still haunted by the memories of my baby brother and sister.

The pain of losing them is still so raw it sometimes feels like it happened only yesterday. And I'm still that little girl, waiting for my brother and sister to come back and find me.

For their sakes, I feel I have a duty to uncover the truth one day.

24

The Future

I HAVE A recurring dream. It's about Mellie and Momo – we're all at Busch Gardens in Virginia, which is a huge amusement park like Disney World.

I went there once with my Nanny and PopPop but I never went with Mellie or Momo in real life. But here we are anyway, in my dream, looking at the different animals together and they're getting really excited about the elephants and lions. I'm the age I am now but Mellie and Momo are still just five and six.

They look really happy until we get to the rides – a giant rollercoaster looms up in front of us, a purple monster snaking up into the sky, looping round and round and soaring to impossible heights so it hurts my neck just to look to the top.

I want to go on the ride – it looks so fun – but Mellie and Momo stop walking. They don't want to get on, it's too scary for them.

I'm urging them to come on the ride with me, dragging them by their reluctant arms as they dig their heels into the ground to stop me from getting them any nearer to the rollercoaster.

They're shaking their heads, adamant they won't climb aboard – Momo's face is scrunched up into a scowl, Mellie is whimpering softly.

I tell them it's going to be okay and they'll be safe with me. But they don't get on the rollercoaster. I'm climbing inside one of the bright red cars that run around the tracks and I'm calling out for them to join me, my arms outstretched and at that point...

I wake up. They never get on the ride with me. Never.

In September 2009 I enrolled in Virginia College for a medical assisting degree to get my nursing qualification. I'm hoping to graduate in 2014 and then get an internship in a maternity hospital so that I can work as a registered nurse with newborns. It's been my dream for as long as I can remember. That first day in college was nerve-racking but so exciting at the same time.

I couldn't believe I was sat there in class, next to all these other students. I'd been so close to dropping out completely it was a source of real pride just to be there at all.

And you know what – with every week that passes I'm doing better and better. I'm still fighting my own insecurities when it comes to my abilities but learning about something I'm really interested in makes it so much easier, and it makes me feel so happy too.

I realise I'm not stupid – I perform as well as any of my classmates when it comes to essays, tests and projects. And I like the social environment too – I've met some good friends already and I feel like I fit in pretty well.

If people ask, I'm not afraid to tell them the truth of what happened to me, my mom and my family but afterwards they always sit back and shake their heads in wonderment.

They're always amazed that I'm as normal as I am and the most frequent reaction is one of admiration: 'You been through all that and you still in school? I know of folk going off the rails for much less!'

I guess I always knew I was strong – but I've tried to take something good from my experiences. My mom showed me how not to live my life but there were plenty of people on the way, like my dad, Theresa and my grandma, who gave me all the tools I needed to stay on the right path

That's not to say that my life is now easy. I have to earn money to put myself through college – when I'm not studying I work in a day care centre for little kids. I love it – being around children is my real joy in life.

I usually go to classes in the day and then work from 3 p.m. till 11 p.m. every weekday. It's quite an intense lifestyle but then I've got to do it because I'm paying my own way.

Looking after children is something I was always

good at, something that came naturally to me, and being in day care is wonderful. I love the sounds and smells of the place. The only thing I don't like is hearing children crying – it sets off bells in my head. If there's a child crying in the day care centre, I'll tear through the place looking for that child and then I can always get them to stop. Even if the child is in another class and doesn't know me. It just takes a few minutes and I'll have them quiet again

There is a lot about what I do which is instinctive but I've also learned a lot about bringing up children and the best way to nurture and encourage them through my work. I've learned that teaching them boundaries and discipline through a firm yet loving framework is the best way of creating confident and happy children.

I've learned that the way you talk and interact with children is vital in making them feel secure and loved. I've learned about firing their imaginations, encouraging their communication skills and helping them develop at every stage.

I hope one day to have children of my own and I'd like to be a good mother to them, give them the stability, love and warmth that I always felt was lacking in my own childhood.

But I'm not in any hurry – I look around and see other girls my age who have had kids and had to give up their dreams and ambitions. There's so much I want to achieve before I settle down. I know that nobody –

not a child or a man – can make me happy. I have to do that myself.

On a day-to-day basis, children do lift my spirits.

I feel comfortable with children where I don't always feel comfortable with adults. Babies and toddlers, they don't judge you. They just love you unconditionally. That simple outlook reminds me there is still a lot of good in the world.

About a year ago, we had a little boy in who was just like my little brother, Mellie. He was the spitting image of him and had the same easy, laid-back personality. I used to wander into his classroom, pick him up and cover him in kisses! I'd baby him so much sometimes he didn't want to go home with his momma because he got used to me cuddling him all the time!

There haven't been any little girls like Momo though. No, she was something else – unique. She had that sassy attitude that told you she was gonna do things her way or not at all! When I think of her it reminds me of myself at that age – we were a pair of troublemakers, big mouths and daredevils!

I'd be surprised if I ever came across another little girl like her in day care

I carry something similar to survivor's guilt when it comes to my brother and sister. Every milestone I pass, I do it without them and it makes me sad that they will never get to share these experiences too. I'll live with that for the rest of my life. One day I'll get married, and they won't; one day I'll have children and they won't.

The guilt doesn't go away – or that feeling of missing them. It only increases because my experiences in the world become deeper, more diverse and meaningful. That's what my rollercoaster dream is all about, the guilt of becoming an adult and enjoying life's experiences without them. Nobody in my family knows how that feels – except maybe Sonny. Still, he was very young when all that happened and he never knew Mellie and Momo. I carry them with me and hold them close because nobody in the world knew them like I did.

As for Sonny, we're getting closer every day. He knows he can always come and talk to me and I would do anything for him. He didn't have a great start in life, but we're family and I hope that he finds his path, like I have.

I still get stressed, I still have racing thoughts and there are times when I feel depressed but I've learned how to deal with these emotions better than before. The one thing that has helped is the realisation that I am not my mother, I am my own person and I have every right to a good and successful future, no matter how difficult my early years.

I refuse to let the past overwhelm me or dictate the person I want to be. Yes, I know where I came from – and I cling to the people and the memories that have shaped my life. But I am not destined to *become* any of them – my mother is chemically unbalanced. I am not.

So when I feel the stresses and strains of life getting to me, I don't turn to alcohol or drugs or anything that will affect the balance of my mind. Instead, I try to calm it.

First I'll turn off my phone then I'll take a cooling shower and go to my room, open the window, turn off the lights and light a couple of candles.

Then I'll lie back on my bed, listen to the birds and meditate. I practise techniques that help calm and clear my mind.

I'm not saying it works for everyone – but it seems to help me a lot. It's helping to keep me on a positive and focused path, one which I hope will lead me to my goals.

On my 21st birthday I got a card from my mom. It was made from yellow card and on the front she'd drawn a birthday cake in blue and pink with orange candles. Ten of them.

The writing on the front was green and spelled out: Happy 21st Birthday.

Inside it read:

Dearest Nikki,

May peace and blessing be upon you. I pray by the time you receive this card you are in great spirits.

Baby girl, I want the best for you. Please get your life on course with the Lord. It took me many years to surrender my will. I am so happy I finally got it together. God is now in charge of my life. Nikki, I want you and your brother to start praying together. I want to be here for you although it's on the phone.

Feel free to tell me any and everything that is going on in your life. Your grandma and me have a good relationship now. We didn't always. Sorry is never too late. I want the best for you. I love you but God loves you more than me. God must come first in your life. It says in the Bible that God is a jealous God. Please put God first in your life. I'm going to end for now but never my love for you.

Love
Mom
xoxoxox

The writing was printed and disjointed – I could tell she was on a lot of medication when she wrote it. It made me happy and sad at the same time. I knew why they'd had to give her more meds that day – she was probably distressed she couldn't be with me on my birthday. But despite everything it didn't stop her from writing to me, even through the blur of the drugs.

In all this time, my mom has written cards and letters to me and I always felt bad that I never wrote back. Until now, that is.

Because this book is the letter I've been planning to write you all this time, Mom.

It's my way of making up for all the years I failed to put down on paper all those things I wanted to say. You wanted to know what was going on in my life, what was going on inside my head – and here are the answers.

I dedicate this book to you.

I hope this goes some way to making up for all the letters and cards I never sent back to you when I know how much you needed to feel my love and hear the truths of my heart.

You waited an awfully long time, 14 years in fact, but I got there in the end! I'm sorry it took me such a long time to let you know that I love you and I'm always thinking about you. It just took a while for me to make sense of all the things that happened to us and though I may not understand everything yet, I do know that I love you.

And I forgive you for what happened to Mellie and Momo.

One day we'll be reunited, facing life together again, hand in hand.

Acknowledgements

I'D LIKE TO THANK...

Katy Weitz for turning my dream into reality – you are an amazing person.

My grandmother and grandfather – the only people who have been there for me since birth and who have never left my side, no matter what. You two are my world and I love you more than words could ever say.

My brothers and sisters – I love you all.

My little brother Hasson – I love you and I'm so happy you are in my life. I want to give you the world!

Uncle Jerome – I love you so much. Thank you for always being there, through the good times and bad. I love you so very much – you are and will always be the greatest in my eyes.

Nanny and PopPop – I love you so much. Thank you.

All my aunts and uncles.

Daddy – I love you. Thank you for doing what you had to do as a father when I needed you. Thank you for making me a responsible, respectful lady. I appreciate you.

Theresa – I love you so much. You are a great

woman. Thank you for everything you have ever done for me. Thank you for being a mother figure for so many years. You are a beautiful, strong person.

My entire family – I love you all!

And a huge thank you to those who have been there for me and helped me in numerous ways throughout the years – I love you and always will no matter what: Mrs Becky, Brandon, Brittany & y'all beautiful loving family and Mrs Jackie.

Johnny – you mean so much to me. I'll always love you.

Carlos, Agatha and Telou. Tammy and Laila.

My best friends Aubern, Ariel and their beautiful babies Donshe, Dion and Jr. – I love you. You are such a blessing in my life.

Momo and Mellie – my angels. I love and miss you two so much. Please continue to watch over me.

Mom, I love you.

And finally, thank you God for your many blessings. I love you above all things!

About the Author

Born in 1991, Nikkia Roberson grew up in Amityville, New York. She now lives in Augusta, Georgia where she is studying to become a nurse and works part-time at a day care centre for children.

Mental Health and the Family

IN THE USA there are now more than 1 million women behind bars for criminal behaviour and the truth is that many of these suffer from mental health problems. As many as 80 per cent of incarcerated women meet the criteria for at least one lifetime psychiatric disorder.

The problem with my mom's illness, schizoaffective disorder, is one of diagnosis: the person displays symptoms which can be misdiagnosed as either a mood disorder like bipolar or a schizophrenic disorder. Nobody knows what causes this illness – it is thought to be a combination of both genetic predisposition and environmental factors. I hope that in time we will learn more from research and science that allows us to recognise and treat those with this illness to prevent further tragedies of the innocent.

My mom is lucky in some ways – her condition has now been diagnosed and she is receiving appropriate care. I only wish she had got the right treatment sooner and that someone in the care system had recognised that with her illness, she was incapable of caring for the children she had created. I wish more people had taken responsibility for us kids when we needed it most – the adults, judges and social workers who decided our fates. I encourage anyone who has any concerns about a child to report it to the proper authorities, no matter what the consequences might be. I urge anyone reading this to realise they have a duty towards every child who crosses their path, to keep them safe from harm, be they family members, friends, neighbours or even strangers.

I've found a great deal of information, support and education online and if you wish to find out more, donate to research or help in raising awareness you can visit a number of different websites:

www.schizophrenia.com
A non-profit source of information, support and education.

www.witnessjustice.org
Provides help and healing for victims of crime.

www.nami.org
The National Alliance on Mental Illness strives to share information with people with mental illness, their families, friends, mental health professionals and the general public.

www.mentalheathamerica.net
Provides a wealth of information, including access to local services and support groups. It is dedicated to

promoting mental health, preventing mental and substance use conditions and achieving victory over mental illnesses and addictions through advocacy, education, research and service.

And in the UK there are these additional resources:

www.mind.org.uk
Mind provides support and advice in the UK across a wide range of services.

www.mentalhealth.org.uk
The Mental Health Foundation uses research and practical projects to help people survive, recover from and avert mental health problems.

www.rethink.org
Rethink Mental Illness offers support and advice for everyone affected by severe mental illness.

www.sane.org.uk
Sane provides information, crisis care and emotional support.

Also by Ebury Press ...

Everybody Knew

A Boy. Two Brothers.
A Stolen Childhood.

MICHAEL CLEMENGER

Michael Clemenger was handed over as a baby to the unloving care of a religious-run children's home. Aged eight, he was transferred to St Joseph's Industrial School. Chosen as their 'favourite' by two Christian Brothers, Michael endured years of sexual abuse at the hands of both men. But despite the unbelievable trauma of his early life, Michael emerged unbroken and determined to make something of himself. *Everybody Knew* is a story of remarkable spirit and courage.

To find out more about our latest publications,
sign up to our newsletter at:
www.eburypublishing.co.uk